Abortion Practice in Britain and the United States

Abortion Practice in Britain and the United States

COLIN FRANCOME

Department of Sociology, Middlesex Polytechnic

London
ALLEN & UNWIN
Boston   Sydney

Allen & Unwin (Publishers) Ltd,
40 Museum Street, London WC1A 1LU, UK

Allen & Unwin (Publishers) Ltd,
Park Lane, Hemel Hempstead, Herts HP2 4TE, UK

Allen & Unwin, Inc.,
8 Winchester Place, Winchester, Mass. 01890, USA

Allen & Unwin (Australia) Ltd,
8 Napier Street, North Sydney, NSW 2060, Australia

First published in 1986

British Library Cataloguing in Publication Data

Francome, Colin
  Abortion practice in Britain and the
  United States.
1. Abortion – Great Britain   2. Abortion
– United States
I. Title
363.4'6'0941   HQ 767.5.G7
ISBN 0-04-179003-0
ISBN 0-04-179004-9 Pbk

Library of Congress Cataloging in Publication Data

Francome, Colin
  Abortion practice in Britain and the United States.
  Bibliography: p.
  Includes index.
1. Abortion – United States.   2. Abortion – Great
Britain.   3. Birth Control – United States.   4. Birth Control
– Great Britain.
I. Title. [DNLM: 1. Abortion, Induced
– trends – Great Britain.   2. Abortion, Induced – trends –
United States.   3. Abortion, Legal – trends – Great Britain.
4. Abortion, Legal – trends – United States.
HQ 767.5.U5 F825a]
HQ 767.5.U5F718 1986   363.4'6'0941   86-3632
ISBN 0-04-179003-0 (alk. paper)
ISBN 0-04-179004-9 (pbk. : alk. paper)

Set in 10 on 12 point Bembo by Columns, Reading
and printed in Great Britain by Billing and Son Ltd,
London and Worcester

Contents

Acknowledgements

During the course of this research I have received help from a number of people. In particular I would like to thank Barbara Apletree who carried out most of the coding of the questionnaires and all of the computer analysis of the results. Other coding was carried out by Donna Carson and myself. Professor Peter Huntingford helped me to make contacts within the British Health Service and was involved with the planning of the research. Uta Landy helped me get respondents in the United States.

In the United States I would also like to thank Bill Baird, Barbara Methvin, Roxanne Feldschuh, Genevieve C. Vieito, Leah Sayles, Joan Henneberry, Linda S. Cooper, Jan Diedrich, Richard Lincoln, Stan Henshaw, Maxine Barrett, Jean E. Raymond, Martin Cohn, Mary Hare, Sue Jacobs, Nancy J. Tolliver, Alan Honorof, Patty Weisenfeld, Maureen Brauch.

In Britain I had help from Diane Munday, Wendy Savage, Joan Andrews, Audrey Ward, Dr Phillip Cauthery, Marion Hall, Peter Diggory, D. B. Paintin, Guy Randle, John McGarry, Roger Baldwin, John Trueman, Bob Francome, Tim Black, Hilary Jackson, Judy Cottam, Avril Francome, Toni Belfield, Kay Wellings, Caroline Francome, Alan Ornstein, Donna Carson, Barbara Nicholls, Marion Newman, Kim Lavely, Fiona Simpson, Ian Jones, Kit McCarthy and Carole Hill, and my editor Gordon Smith who advised me throughout.

Finally I would like to thank Ann Morris who regularly let me in to type before the College was officially open and Alison Banks, Sylvia Lambrinos, Suzy Atteck and Anna Kyprianou who shared the word processors with me.

The research was supported by the Marie Stopes Research Fund.

List of Abbreviations

AGI   Alan Guttmacher Institute
BMA   British Medical Association
BMJ   *British Medical Journal*
BPAS British Pregnancy Advisory Service
FPIS Family Planning Information Service
NHS   National Health Service
NYT   *New York Times*
OPCS Office of Population Censuses and Surveys
RCOG Royal College of Obstetricians and Gynaecologists

1 Introduction

The average rate of abortions in the United States is more than twice that for Britain. This book will examine the reasons for this difference and also consider ways in which the abortion rates in both countries can be reduced. The general strategy on this issue has been a matter of controversy. On one side are those such as the Festival of Light in Britain and the Moral Majority in the United States who argue that the solution to the unwanted pregnancy is to encourage chastity. They have criticised the birth control advocates whom they see as encouraging greater sexuality and by this means making the problem of unwanted pregnancies worse. A clear statement of this viewpoint was made by Archbishop Bernadin in the *New York Times*. On the fifth anniversary of the Supreme Court's decision legalising abortion, he said he doubted whether 'more and better contraceptive information and services will make major inroads in the number of teenage pregnancies – it will motivate them to precocious sexual activity but by no means to the practice of contraception. In which case the solution will merely have made the problem worse' (22 January 1978). On the other side, this kind of argument is criticised by the family planning providers who in recent years have been able to point to some successes. In particular, the rate of teenage births in Britain has declined: for every five in 1970 there were only three in 1980. Less than one-seventh of this reduction was due to an increase in abortions (Francome, 1984b), and there does not seem to have been a lessening of teenage sexual activity, which indicates that the extension of birth control facilities was being effective in reducing unwanted pregnancies.

However, the evidence for both countries also shows great gaps of knowledge and suggests that even greater improvements could be made in terms of reducing the number of unwanted pregnancies and abortions. In the United States in particular, the level of birth control provision and use is so low – with less than a quarter of our sample always using birth control – that a realistic target could be to expand facilities and halve the abortion rate over a five-year period. In Britain, two in five of our sample of women seeking abortions had been using birth control at the time of conception. While this research will make it clear that it is not only birth control differences that lead to the variations in the abortion rate, the evidence to be presented will suggest that an improvement of services and improved sex education could lead to a 25 per cent drop in abortions over the same period.

The Structure of the Book

The book is evenly divided in the attention it pays to Britain and the United States. In the next two chapters the historical evidence on abortion is considered. As my main aim is to deal with the current sitation, these chapters are relatively brief. In terms of other contributions in the area, Potts, Diggory and Peel (1977) have discussed abortion in nineteenth-century Britain and Madeleine Simms (1975) has produced useful work on the situation in the 1930s. In the United States there have been some useful histories (Means, 1968, 1971; Mohr, 1978; Luker, 1984) and other authors more concerned with birth control also mention abortion (Gordon, 1977; Reed, 1978). I attempt to draw the major findings together and to estimate the frequency of abortion at different periods.

There are those in Britain and the United States who call for a return to nineteenth-century values – the implication being that the great repression of sexuality in that period led to more people being chaste and sexual problems being much less common. The evidence presented in these chapters, however, shows that in nineteenth-century Britain sexual problems were so great that many parents had children they could not care for or sought abortions either by means of pills or by abortionists working illegally. It seems that the British abortion rate was highest in the period before the First World War. In the United States, birth control use has been consistently less than in Britain and the abortion rate has always been higher. Indeed, it was often stated to be the highest in the world. These two historical chapters lead up to the introduction of liberal laws in both countries and they imply that an open approach could be more successful in curing sexual problems.

In Chapters 4 and 5 I consider the experience of legal abortion in Britain since 1968 and in the United States since 1970. I present the official data before discussing the original data of this research, which are largely based on a survey of 1,129 women in the United States and 649 in Britain who were at hospitals or clinics to have abortions between 1982 and 1984. The same questionnaire was used in each country. These chapters look at birth control at the early stages of intercourse and some of the related cultural phenomena such as the relationship between men and women. They also consider birth control use at the time of conception and the effects of such factors as marital status, religious and ethnic groups. The comparative data on repeat abortions are also considered. At the end of the British chapter the Scottish data are investigated further. The United States chapter has a separate section on men's attitude to birth control and abortion. In Chapter 6, the abortion rates in Britain and the United States are compared, with extra attention being paid to the differences between teenagers. The comparative use of birth control is also considered as are differences in discussion with parents and siblings. In assessing the reasons for the differences in abortion rate, special attention is paid to cultural factors, particularly where young people are concerned. In the Conclusion I suggest some of the changes in social policy that are indicated by this research.

How the research was done

The general problems of social research are accentuated in the area of sexuality because it is such a taboo-laden subject. This book will show that people often do not discuss their personal problems even with their most intimate friends and relations. While researchers do have the advantage of anonymity to gain information, it is often not easy to get to the truth. So it is important to use a variety of different sources and so build up a more accurate picture of the situation. In this research, four separate kinds of information were used.

First of all, much published data are available either from official sources such as the British Office of Population Censuses and Surveys (OPCS) or from places partially financed by the state such as the Alan Guttmacher Institute (AGI) in New York. The figures from such sources give an overall perspective against which more detailed analysis can occur and they also provide data for international comparisons. Furthermore, they enabled me to make comparisons between the samples in this study and the overall characteristics of women having abortions.

Secondly, and in some respects most importantly, data were collected from 1,129 women having abortions in the United States and 649 in Britain. Because British society is relatively more highly integrated, it is possible to get a representative sample with fewer respondents. The same questionnaire was used for both samples (see the Appendix). It was based on the questions asked in a previous survey and was self-administered (Francome and Francome, 1979). This had the advantage of anonymity but the disadvantage that recent immigrants sometimes had difficulty with the language. One London hospital reported that it handled 10–12 patients a week, approximately half of whom were born outside the country and about 10 per cent of whom had very limited English. So some of the questionnaires were only partially completed and there was a different response rate for various questions. In tabulating the results I have made clear the exact number of responses in each case.

The samples in the two societies were constructed somewhat differently, reflecting in part the fact that the operation is carried out under different conditions. In Britain, I made a deliberate attempt to get respondents from the three main groups of abortion providers – the National Health Service (NHS), the charities and the private sector. Peter Huntingford, who was at the time Professor of Obstetrics at the London Hospital, lent his support to the project and signed a joint letter with me to various NHS consultants in different parts of the country. Those co-operating were asked to give the questionnaire to consecutive patients during a specified period. In most cases the consultants gave the questionnaires to the women at time of the examination and arranged for them to be collected anonymously. Sometimes, however, the questionnaires were given out and collected by counsellors. In Scotland, the questionnaires were given out by the doctors but the women were given prepaid envelopes to post them back to me. Questionnaires were received from eight NHS sampling points. Two charities cooperated with the survey, including the largest in the country – the British Pregnancy Advisory Service (BPAS). A letter went out from the director asking for support and questionnaires were obtained from all the BPAS clinics. Part of the letter from the director Ian Jones read as follows:

> The idea is to give a copy of the enclosed letter and questionnaire to consecutive abortion patients attending the nursing home each day for a specified period of 1 week commencing 21 May 1984 and asking those patients that do complete the questionnaire to place it in a 'post box' for anonymity at some time during their stay. It would only be used for residents of England, Wales and Scotland and would apply equally to day and overnight cases. There is no need to follow up patients to complete the forms, simply distribute them with some encouragement and collect the outcome. Keep a record of the number of forms given out and the number of non respondents can then be stated.

This was also the procedure usually followed in the private sector. The questionnaires were given out by counsellors and a box was positioned centrally for women to drop in their responses.

In the United States I contacted Dr Uta Landy, who was at the time Executive Director of the National Abortion Federation. She wrote to her members suggesting they should contact me if they were interested in participating in the study. In the end twelve centres helped with the study and they were from all parts of the country. The fact that hospitals were not included in the sample probably meant that it contained a smaller proportion of those having Medicaid abortions and that there was an over-representation of the better-off groups. However, this is not likely to have affected the overall conclusions of the book.

The response rate was generally very good. One factor that affects it is clearly the presentation of the questionnaire to the patient. Previous surveys have shown that where the medical profession has been involved in encouraging patients to co-operate there can be a nearly 100 per cent response (Jackson, 1984). In Britain, many of the organising NHS consultants reported total co-operation from patients. The response rate in the private sector and charities varied somewhat according largely to the encouragement given by staff, but overall was estimated at 82 per cent. The response rate in the United States was slightly higher: information from my contacts at the individual clinics indicates an overall response rate of over 90 per cent, and the director of one centre told me that she had received a questionnaire back from each of the 130 women given it. The fact that in the United States day care was commonly used meant that for many of the women the filling in of the questionnaire was just one of the things they did during that day. However, the British respondents showed more reflection and were more likely to have added further comments outside the bare questions asked. It is the information from this statistical work that provides a major part of the data in this book.

A third source of data was interviews of various kinds. First of all there were unstructured interviews conducted at abortion clinics. Thirty of these took place in the United States with males accompanying their partners who were having abortions and many of these are taped. There were also some with the women themselves. These interviews discussed various relevant issues about the extent of birth control use. I found it an advantage to be from another country as my interviewees were happy to talk about the subject and ther feelings in the light of my intention to make cross-cultural comparisons. I also conducted interviews with people I was directed to by a network of contacts. A good example is the interview reported in Chapter 5, pp. 129–31. On other occasions my discussions with people would raise points of interest that might lead to a formal interview at another time. I also instituted some group interviews and discussions on the subject of the menstrual period, which had produced results I was not expecting. These interviews provided useful background information which could not easily be gleaned from the reading of the questionnaires on their own.

The fourth source of data was direct involvement in the culture – known to sociologists as participant observation. One of the reasons for the differences in abortion rates between Britain and the United States is the contrasts in the youth cultures of the two societies. In this research I have drawn on my previous data in this area. In my earlier research into youth culture I had observed a British peer group over a seven-year period, 1969–76 (Francome, 1976a). This group of more than twenty teenagers called itself 'Allenbrooke' after 'Allenbrooke Crescent', Swindon, a road near to where they lived. I had access to the group as the elder brother of one of the members. This research provided me with much detailed insight into the nature of British peer groups and the way in which reported behaviour compared and contrasted with the reality of the situation. In particular it gave me information about the relationship between the sexes and the way that young men often over-stated their sexual activity while young women under-stated it. This is an important point to which I shall return. In recent years my relationship with the British youth culture has been more as an observer than as a participant, but I have kept in touch with developments through in-depth discussions with teenagers and through the work of other academics.

When I taught in the United States for a year, 1977–8, I observed the behaviour of the young in the United States and studied the relevant differences. I also carried out an attitude survey of 1,000 students at a Long Island Community College which in part dealt with sexual matters (see p. 177). With these data I have been able to build up a picture of comparisons between the countries.

In all, the aim has been to bring together information from a variety of sources and weld it into a coherent picture.

How accurate are research data?

When carrying out sex research, one of the questions of importance is the degree of accuracy it is possible to obtain. From my research over the years I have come to the conclusion that there are very real problems in getting accurate data in the face of very strong cultural taboos. In particular, where there is a double standard there will be a tendency for men to over-state their sexual activity and for women to under-state it. The early researchers recognised this; Kinsey *et al.*, for example, reported:

> Comparisons of the frequency data for premarital coitus reported by the females and males in the sample show discrepancies of considerable magnitude. Quite consistently in every educational level and for every age group the males reported incidence and frequencies which were higher and in some cases considerably higher than those reported by the females. [1953, p.80]

Kinsey found that, even excluding intercourse with prostitutes, in the age group 16–20 males said they had seven times as much premarital intercourse as females. Men aged 21–25 claimed to have had four times as much intercourse as equivalent women. However, the most remarkable figures came from boys in the under-16 group. They claimed to have intercourse four times as often as women aged 16–20 and even twice as often as those aged 21–25. Kinsey concluded that the women covered up part of their sexual activity (1953, p.79,80).

The first study in Britain to use random sampling for a teenage sex survey (Schofield, 1965) similarly found that the male teenagers claimed to have more sex than the female ones. In the age group 15–19 the boys claimed four times as many sexual partners as the girls despite the fact that they tended to date girls younger than them and that the younger women claimed to have less sex than the older ones. Schofield suggested the discrepancies were due to 'highly promiscuous girls not represented in our sample' (p.244). However, on the basis of participant observation I offer an alternative explanation, which is that there is a consistent tendency for both sexes to misrepresent events in order to protect themselves or gain status within the culture.

One reason why men should have over-stated their sexuality is given in the classic work on British coalminers:

> Any display of tenderness or affection seems to be regarded as 'soft'. If one of the group of young males at this early

stage does begin to take a girl seriously he finds himself the butt of consistent 'kidding'. Only a convincing and jealousy-provoking claim that he is intimate with his girlfriend will save him from ridicule' [Dennis, Henriques and Slaughter, 1956, p.222]

So peer group pressure is one factor and this was certainly found in my research too. In my earlier research I reported the comments of a 19-year-old youth commenting on his behaviour a few years previously: 'After we'd all taken girls home on a Saturday night, we'd get together and ask each other, "Did you have it last night?" and we'd all claim to, whereas really none of us had' (Francome, 1976a, p.155).

In general such facts as self-image, the need to maintain face and concern with long-term reputation affect people's interpretation of events. In my research I have found that it is casual sex that is least likely to be accurately reported. I will give just one example from my records. In the summer of 1976 I was at a discotheque in Spain with a small group. A cockney-born mathematics student met an English girl and suddenly left with her very early in the evening without even saying goodbye to anyone. He returned about an hour and a half later and there was some banter about why he had returned. He replied, 'I've had my oats already' – a point that came under some dispute from his close friends on the grounds of his early return. However, he claimed that he had returned because he did not rate her very highly and 'anyway she was only 17'. A few days later I began talking to the girl and her companion and she told a different story. She said of the boy, 'Your friend is really horrible and only thinks of sex. He even wanted to have it with me although I am only 15.' Furthermore, she said when she refused he went away and left her.

This evidence is relevant to my analysis here for a number of reasons. First of all the double standard and the games between the sexes can be a crucial factor in non-use of birth control. In casual sex there is less commitment to the partner's longer-term wellbeing. Secondly it shows the need not to accept responses simply at their face value but to dig more deeply. In terms of the accuracy of this survey I believe that some of the males presented the age at their first intercourse as lower than it actually was. However, an advantage of this current research is that the respondents were clearly sexually active and so there was not the same conflict in terms of admitting sexuality. Furthermore, my use of participant observation leads me to doubt the findings of sex surveys based on interviews that men start their sexual activity earlier than women and have more sex as teenagers than women.

It has become clear to me over the years that the fact that the culture has been more likely to applaud male sexuality has led to confusion. Hollingshead, in his participant observation of *Elmstown Youth* (1949), for example, found that more girls were having sex than boys; yet he concluded that his sample must have been unrepresentative: 'Although the few figures given here involve about four times as many girls as boys, we do not want to give the impression that high school girls are more likely to have sex relations than boys. The contrary is the case, as Kinsey has indicated' (1961, p.239). Now I take the view that Hollingshead's respondents were not particularly unusual and that this is what normally happens. Given that women are more likely to date older men than vice versa it is only logical that their average age of first sex should be lower. My research found that women having abortions were on average much younger than their partners. Furthermore, certain objective data also point in the same direction. In Britain, Schofield (1965) for example found that overall three times as many men contracted gonorrhoea as women. However, amongst the under-sixteens girls were three times as likely to become infected as boys and they also predominated in the 16–17 age group (Schofield, 1965, p.114). Similarly, we know that unmarried mothers are more likely to be teenagers than are unmarried fathers (Wimperis, 1960). These facts point to women starting sex at a younger age. Similarly in most of the American states some recognition of the differing ages of maturity is indicated in the fact that women can marry at the age of 15 compared to 18 for the men. So I suggest that some myths have grown up over the years and a clearer understanding of comparative sexuality will enable us to make our social policy more relevant.

Note on terminology

People dealing with data from the British Isles have to cope with several bases for statistics. For most purposes the figures for England and Wales are given separately from those for Scotland. If these three countries are counted together, the data are reported as being for 'Britain'. For most purposes I have produced the survey results for the whole of the British sample. There is a problem in terms of identifying a transference time when girls and boys should be referred to as men and women. Some use puberty as the time to change the terminology, but there is a cultural difference in that in Britain the term 'boy' or 'girl' can be used of any age in certain circumstances without it being offensive to the vast majority. For example, the day before I wrote this section I was in conversation with a long-time activist whose 87-year-old husband is a life Peer. In discussing his activities she called him a 'naughty boy' because he sometimes refused to obey the Labour Whip in the House of Lords. This use of the word would be much more unusual in the United States. I have attempted to maintain a degree of flexibility rather than talk of 14-year-old men and women.

2 The Development of Abortion Practice in Britain to 1967

Before the nineteenth century the law in Britain allowed abortion until quickening – the time when movement could be felt in the womb (about 15 weeks gestation). Parry translates a commentary published about 1290 on the law in force at the time: 'The woman commits homicide, who by potions and drugs of that sort, shall have destroyed her animate child in her womb' (1932, p.95). The law also said that anyone who had overlain a pregnant woman or given her drugs or blows to procure abortion was committing homicide. (Quickening was an important legal concept and no woman could be executed if she had passed the quickening stage, so a special jury of women was formed to feel the prisoner's stomach and determine whether there was movement.)

Nineteenth-century abortion legislation

Parry suggests that it was a common practice for women who were going to have an illegitimate baby to kill it after birth and say it had been born dead (p.96). The law was therefore very harsh on women who concealed their pregnancy. Although Ellenborough's 1803 Act made abortion illegal at all stages of pregnancy, it was in part an attempt to redress the balance between infanticide and abortion. A portion of *The Times* report quoted Ellenborough as saying that the law was too severe in its attitude to an unmarried mother whose child dies and 'The proof of the mother having previously concealed her pregnancy, is taken as sufficient to convict of murder' (29 March 1803). The Act repealed this section of the law and said that trials in such cases should proceed by the rules of evidence governing other cases. Another crucial factor in the law seems to have been concern over the dangers of abortion to women.

There seems to have been a curious omission from the Act, however. The *Lancet* commented:

> That Act made the attempt to Procure abortion by means of instrument when the woman was not quick with child or could not be proved to be so, a misdemeanour; but by singular omission, left the case of attempting to procure abortion by instrument, when the woman was quick with child, unprovided for [11 April 1829]

The *Lancet* went on to say that the administration of a 'noxious or destructive substance' for the same purpose was made a capital felony. The *Lancet* argued that it was this loophole that allowed doctors to perform abortion to save a woman's life.

As far as illegal abortions were concerned, the law did not seem to have much effect, and four years after the Act an advertisement in *Bells Court and Fashionable Magazine* (September 1807) stated:

> Lost happiness regained – any lady of respectability involved in distress from any expectation of inevitable dishonour, may obtain consolation and security and a real friend in the hour of anxiety and peril by addressing a line (post paid) to Mrs Grimston, No 18 Broad Street Golden Square, when a private interview with the advertiser will be appointed. Ladies thus situated may depend on the strictest secrecy and motherly attention, combined with every comfort so necessary on these occasions for the restoration of that serenity of mind generally attendant on the cultivated life. [*Lancet*, 21 May 1932]

There does not seem to have been any move against such advertisements.

The first trial under the Act did not occur until 1811, when a man was charged with giving a single woman a concoction made by pouring boiled water over the leaves of a shrub called savin. This was said to be a 'noxious and destructive thing'. He, however, successfully argued that she had threatened to commit suicide unless able to conceal her shame and that he had therefore given her the mixture to amuse her (Parry, 1932).

As indicated, the medical profession in the early part of the century seems to have carried out abortion in some cases where the woman was ill. The first reference I found to this was in 1828 and it tells something of the medical practice of the time. A woman five and a half months pregnant was very ill after the shock of the house next door catching on fire. The doctor John Holmes was very worried about her:

> I stated my opinion that nothing could be done but to bring on premature labour. The doctor (consulting) assented and I then suggested the use of ergot of rye; and if that failed the necessity of puncturing the membranes. This was agreed to, and on the same day (Saturday) I proceeded to bring on labour. For this purpose I administered about half past eleven o'clock a wine glassful of infusion of ergot of rye (made by infusing ziij of ergot in half pint of boiling water). [*Lancet*, 20 September 1828]

He went on to say that to complete the abortion he had to perforate the membranes and he stressed the value of ergot of rye in such cases.

However it seems that some doctors were not even carrying out abortion to save the woman's life and shortly after this case the *Lancet* (11 April 1829) published an editorial complaining that the 1803 Act was being interpreted too narrowly and that a woman had died as a result of trying to produce an abortion by medicines and an operation. It continued to complain that if the loophole in Ellenborough's Act was closed then doctors carrying out abortions for good reasons could risk being hanged. However, the loophole was removed that year by an Act introduced by Lord Lansdowne. The penalty for aborting a woman 'quick' with child was to be death. For a woman in the earlier part of pregnancy it was to be transportation for seven to fourteen years or imprisonment for up to three years with the possibility of a public whipping (Parry, 1932). The sentences for abortion were reduced in the Offences Against the Person Act 1837: the death sentence was abolished and the maximum prison sentence became three years. Despite the concern of the *Lancet* in 1829, legal abortions to save the woman's life continued. Indeed, the *Provincial Medical and Surgical Journal* (1852, p.323) welcomed the fact that the French, despite being under the influence of the 'Romish religion' and having opposed the death of the foetus and imperilled the woman's life to the last degree, were now discussing the issue.

As far as illegal abortion is concerned, savin was mentioned in 1837 as being the most commonly used method and was often successful. Professor Thompson thought abortion was rare but that it occurred more amongst the working classes: 'Should pregnancy in the unmarried female of rank take place, the disgrace can more easily be concealed; but in the middling and the lower ranks it occasionally happens that drastic purgatives are taken to procure abortion' (*Lancet*, 28 January 1837). Other doctors began to argue, however, that abortion was common. One wrote to the *Provincial Medical and Surgical Journal* that he had attended three young women who had aborted themselves with herbs in the previous eighteen months. He suggested that such cases were constantly occurring and increasing, and further commented:

Can we feel surprised, as in the case of a girl who has yielded to her seducer, rather than be immured probably for a life time in the dreaded union house, she should stifle her better feelings and relieve herself of a burden, when this can be effected simply by taking drugs, which she has no idea will be injurious to her constitution. [*Provincial Medical and Surgical Journal*, 1844, p.81]

By the 1850s, apart from the use of herbs there was also evidence of people working as illegal abortionists. The *Lancet* devoted an editorial to the subject, asking:

Who can tell what is going on beneath the turbid and seething surfaces of society, especially in the ranks below that section which acts under the influences of conventional proprieties . . . Can we conceal from ourselves that if the practice of procuring criminal abortion be pursued as a trade that it is carried out to a frightful extent. [21 May 1853]

A few months later (30 July), the *Lancet* returned to the subject and told of handbills addressed to female domestics telling them how they could get abortions.

It seems that some doctors were also carrying out abortions, for in the same year the *Association Medical Journal* deplored the fact that the medical colleges could not rid itself of those performing them (13 May 1853). In the 1861 the *Lancet* published another editorial on the subject, stating that abortion had become a money-making activity carried out by both sexes (23 March). Also in 1861 the Offences Against the Person's Act continued the prohibition on abortion but said that the attempt should not be made 'unlawfully' which implied that in some cases lawful attempts at abortion could be made (Francome, 1984a, p.30, 209, 210).

'Baby Farming and Baby Murder' (1868)

The above was the title of a major investigative series conducted by the *British Medical Journal* (BMJ) into abortion, infanticide and adoption. Women would often pay a person a sum of around £5.00 to adopt their children and raise them in 'baby farms'. One estimate in the 1860s was that each year more than 30,000 children were placed in the hands of baby farmers (Acton, 1878, p.281). The BMJ answered advertisements in various newspapers which undertook to receive ladies 'temporarily indisposed'. However it made clear that investigators kept to the better-quality establishments:

> We have not groped into the darker mysteries of the more infamous quarters of London. We have not followed up clues which have been offered to us by persons who have reason to believe that, among the more abandoned classes of women, there exists a secret understanding as to the persons and places where abortion is practised as a daily trade. [*BMJ*, 22 February 1868]

The first report told of a physican who could be relied upon for accuracy and honour presenting himself at the door of a neat house in a quiet street. He was told that if the lady were too far gone the baby could be adopted and sent into the country for payment of a good sum. However, if the lady was not too far gone the affair could be managed for a larger sum but with perfect safety. The woman proprietor continued to say that the abortion would not harm the woman's health as much as going full term would and commented it was 'hard that people could not have a little enjoyment without being put to such inconvenience afterwards' (*BMJ*, 8 February 1868). The same issue told of another woman who charged 50 guineas for the doctor and 20 for her own services. This woman said the lady could keep her face veiled if she liked and that she had never brought on an abortion without a doctor. The report went on to say that the woman had been in the business for twenty-seven years, was never short of patients, and that some had gone back to her six or seven times. It quoted her: 'I'm a jokelar [jocular] person, I am; and I says funny things and cheers 'em up. She needn't mind, and mustn't fret, and I'll see her all right. I'm the old original, I am, and have had hundreds' (*BMJ*, 8 February 1868).

At another place the reporters tried to find out if there were any time restrictions. On being told the lady was five months pregnant he said he would not mind bringing her on if she had not quickened. This was an interesting point because legally the distinction had disappeared thirty years previously. The reporter commented:

> The impression this man gave me was, that if the lady came, he would administer some drug; and, if it had a certain effect, well and good; if not, then he would not like to resort to further measures; and that to ease his conscience, he would endeavour to justify the use of drugs by assuming the lady had not quickened. [*BMJ*, 22 February 1868]

In all, the investigators visited seven places and in only one was abortion not available. In two of the places there was evidence of infanticide. In one, the woman told them that if the young lady would give birth she would dispose of the child by neglecting it. In the second place there had been seven infant deaths registered in two years.

The *BMJ* attacked the ladies having abortions in part for setting a bad example to their maids (Francome, 1984a, p.32). It also attacked adoption which often occurred without the husband's knowledge. One woman told the journal she frequently had mock births:

> She managed it this way. She arranged with a person who wanted a child, and she went without stays and made herself

look big; then when she had got a suitable child, the person feigned labour, and she went to see them as nurse or midwife, and took the child, to whom she administered half a drop of laudanum to keep it quiet. She takes a great bottle of bullock's blood, which she gets from the butchers, and very often an after birth as well, and then can make as much mess as she likes. The person she went to two days ago took one thirteen months ago; but that was a girl and she wanted a boy as well so she took her one. The person had had no child of her own and thought she and her husband would be more happy if they had children . . . If her husband said anything about having a second child so soon, she would say that the second one came before its time. [*BMJ*, 8 February 1868].

The report was very revealing of Victorian sexual practices, for the BMJ expressed no surprise at the fact that the father could be deceived but rather complained at the transgression of the laws of primogeniture.

In 1877 the Bradlaugh/Besant trial brought contraception to the forefront of public discussion. In 1876 Annie Besant and Charles Bradlaugh, a Bristol bookseller, challenged the law by republishing the booklet 'The Fruits of Philosophy', which gave practical details about birth control. It was written by an American doctor, Charles Knowlton, and had first been published in 1832. Besant and Bradlaugh were initially convicted of obscenity and sentenced to two years' hard labour, but in 1877 they won the appeal. The great publicity led to 125,000 copies of the pamphlet being sold in the first four months after the acquittals and to increased sales of appliances (Francome, 1984a, pp.35–7). However, it does not seem to have reduced the demand for abortion. There is evidence that by 1880 some doctors were carrying out legal abortions on wide grounds. At a meeting of the London Obstetrical Society, a Dr Priestley said that the conditions for the induction of abortion had never been laid down sufficiently clearly. He said it was usual to say that each case should be judged on its merits but that this could lead to serious abuse. Examples had repeatedly come to his knowledge where abortion had been carried out for reasons that seemed to him inadequate. One such was when a woman had once miscarried and feared a second pregnancy might interfere with an important journey (*BMJ*, 1 January 1881). Three years later, the *Lancet* commented that the strongest evidence should be forthcoming before a doctor was brought to account for carrying out the operation or even for the death of his patient, for 'Even if a medical practitioner is known to have procured abortion, the presumption is that it was done in the legal exercise of his calling' (29 March 1884). On the whole, it seems that those carrying out the abortions were a few physicians of high status and that rich members of London society could already get their abortions done legally.

The abortion age, 1896–1914

There are good reasons for believing that this period was the one more than any other in British history when abortion was used or attempted. The evidence for this comes from several sources. There were letters on the subject in the *BMJ* (17 September and 1 October 1898) and in that year too the Chrimes trial led to the *Lancet* campaign against abortifacient advertisements. The *Lancet* attempted to shame the papers by naming those with advertisements and nearly 200 were reported. In 1893 a woman died of lead poisoning and by the early twentieth century many women were using lead pills as abortifacients. In some areas, women of childbearing age were routinely examined for a blue line on their gums, which was indicative of lead poisoning (Francome, 1984a, p.33).

In many ways the best source of information about the practice of abortion was the book *Report on the English Birthrate* by Ethel Elderton (1914) based on the North of England. The evidence was obtained largely by writing to various medical correspondents under the auspices of the Eugenics Society. Elderton was concerned with the decline in the rate of population growth and blamed the Bradlaugh/Besant trial. She argued that this legitimised birth control and so reduced the pressure on population which 'carried the English population as the great colonising force into every quarter of the globe' (p.235). She thought later centuries might see the trial as the death knell of the British Empire. She also mentioned the decline in the trade boom and the reduction of hours during which children could work.

Her report did not, however, show much evidence of birth control; rather it was abortion that women were using in a desperate attempt to control their fertility. In Bradford, for example, the birthrate had fallen from 24.9 per 100 married women aged 15–55 in 1851 to 13.8 in 1901. Her correspondent commented: 'There is a good deal of abortion practised in this district and for every case that comes to notice there are hundreds that do not.' Elderton argued that Leeds was a great centre for fertility control and that many Leeds suppliers advertised the sale of abortifacients and the distribution of birth control information. Her fullest analysis, however, was of the practices in the City of York, where she had three correspondents. Women sometimes asked their doctors for a drug to correct a slight irregularity and then took a large dose. Others used the many pills available in the town – Widow Welch's female pills, Coloynth, steel pills and a common remedy of gin and gunpowder. Evidence was also provided by several wives. One whose husband was often ill and earned 24s a week commented:

> Six out of ten working women take something, if it is only paltry stuff . . . one tells another. There's no hawking here; it's all done in secrecy . . . sometimes they can take a druggist's shop and it does no good . . . the child comes out just the same; but it's puny, it's half starved . . . I knew a child nine months only weighed about four pounds; they kept it alive the twelve month then it died. The mother died too . . . she been taking all sorts, and she went into rapid consumption . . . Our folk go on taking what weakens them, and they can't make up for it like the rich. One woman said to me 'I'd rather swallow the druggist shop and the man in't than have another kid'. [Elderton, 1914, p.136]

Two other working women 'of most respectable type' estimated that at least seven but probably eight out of ten working women took drugs:

> They'll rise money for that, if they rise it for nothing

else . . . the working class are equally bad, bad as the rich . . . I think nearly all of them have a try . . . and there's many that half poison themselves . . . You'll hear them talking 'Oh, I ain't going to have any more I knows summat'. [p.137]

Elderton suggested that while her best evidence was for York she had no doubt it was representative of a wide range of towns. In Birkenhead, for example, she reported:

Women of all classes will ask doctors frankly as to the best methods of prevention and whether they are injurious to health, and also of the best and safest method of abortion . . . Women will frankly state how they avoid pregnancy and recount how they have tried everything to bring an undesired pregnancy to a premature end. Bitter apple, lead plaster, nutmegs, etc. have been taken in many cases with acute symptoms; a few cases have been reported of attempts to introduce knitting needles into the uterus in order to produce abortion. Advertised pills are much tried. [p.80]

Elderton reported that the only place where the birthrate had not fallen was Liverpool and she put this down to the influence of the Irish. Her book was given extensive coverage in the *BMJ* (26 December 1914) and also in the *Malthusian* (January 1915), the main journal supporting birth control at the time. It is likely that it was her research that led to the *Malthusian*'s estimate that 100,000 working women took abortifacient pills each year (May 1914). The *Malthusian* also attacked the 'conspiracy of silence' that kept poor women in ignorance of harmless contraceptive devices and led them to take dangerous drugs (January 1915).

Similar evidence was provided by witnesses to the Birth-Rate Commission, although one witness suggested that the richer groups were using birth control and that about one in four women procured abortion (Birth-Rate Commission, 1917, pp.279–80).

The mistiming of the safe period

There were a number of reasons for the great number of abortions just before the First World War. One was that the neo-Malthusians, in linking birth control to population, provoked the ire of the socialists active in the working-class movement (Francome, 1984a, pp.42–6). Rising expectations was another factor and in the wake of the Bradlaugh/Besant trial people knew it was possible to control births. Poverty, the introduction of full-time education in 1870 and the restrictions on child labour were obviously other relevant factors. However, an important problem was that at this time virtually everyone believed that conception was most likely around the time of the menstrual period.

The view seems to have been based on the work of a German scientist, Thedor Bischoff, who in 1853 published his discovery about eggs in the genital tract of dogs 'on heat' and concluded that women must also ovulate at the time of menstruation. Annie Besant (1877) popularised this view in her work and Elderton (1914) commented primly 'Most women in the country districts know that a human is more likely to be impregnated at a period around the time of menstruation and a great many avoid this time when sober'. After the war, Marie Stopes published the wrong safe period in her best-selling book *Married Love* (1918). This false information was obviously important to Catholics who had received permission to use the safe period in 1853 and whose priests widely quoted the false information (Francome, 1984c).

The Chief Rabbi cast doubt on this view in 1917 because observant Jews, who had no intercourse until twelve days after the start of the menstrual period, did not have smaller families than non-observant Jews (Birth-Rate Commission, 1917). However, the first time people really had strong information was in 1925 when a study by Siegal was reported in Britain. He studied 320 German soldiers and their wives after the men had been home on leave for periods of two–eight days. He found his sample was 'most prolific' six days after the start of the menstrual cycle – somewhat earlier than is now known to be the case, but significantly he found no conceptions after twenty-one days of the cycle. The journal of the neo-

Malthusians commented that his work 'proves beyond question that there is some truth in the doctrine of the safe period, and it also proves that this period comes later in the cycle than is commonly supposed' (New Generation, January 1925, p.10). It was not until the early 1930s that the cycle was fully understood.

Abortion after the First World War

During the First World War a dispute amongst the neo-Malthusians involving H. G. Wells led to an agreement that propaganda for birth control should be spread without reference to doctrines on overpopulation. One of the key activists was Marie Stopes, who was initially a neo-Malthusian but let her membership lapse and began fighting birth control as a single-issue campaign. In 1921 she opened the first birth control clinic in Britain (Francome, 1984a). The growth of birth control can be gauged by the figures in Table 2.1. The results show that the middle classes were the first to adopt birth control but that by 1920–4 manual workers were slightly more likely to be users than were the non-manual. The effect of increasing contraceptive use on demand for abortion can be complicated. At first, expectations of control may rise faster than birth control use, so both birth control and abortion can rise together. However, once birth control becomes more efficient, demand is likely to fall. One observer between the wars, Mr Beckwith Whitehouse, concluded that, overall, birth control had reduced the number of abortions:

Contraceptive measures are undoubtedly one factor in lowering the incidence of the demand for abortion, and within recent years I have been rather impressed with the attitude of mind of the woman who has practised contraception and who has failed to obtain her object. Such a woman instinctively seems to feel that she has the right to demand the termination of an unwanted pregnancy. [Whitehouse, 1932, p.338]

I would suggest that the number of abortions between the wars was somewhat lower than immediately before the First

Table 2.1 Year of marriage and birth control use

Year	Non-manual workers	Skilled workers	Other manual workers	All
Before 1910	26%	18%	4%	15%
1910–19	60%	39%	33%	40%
1920–4	56%	60%	54%	58%

Source: Royal Commission on Population (1949).

World War. The number of deaths was 400–500 every year from 1926 to 1935 but then fell away somewhat until just before the Second World War (Birkett, 1939). Of course, only a small proportion of abortions led to illness. The *Lancet* for example published the records of a Professor Grotjahn who in one year performed 427 abortions with none of his patients having any injury (January 1932).

The main methods of getting an abortion between the wars were similar to those previously practised. We have seen that by the 1880s doctors in London were giving abortions to rich women, and this continued. The fact that a barrister's wife was given abortion on request was discussed openly at the section of obstetrics at the annual meeting of the British Medical Association (BMA) in 1926 (*BMJ*, 7 August). There was no attempt at secrecy, but rather a discussion of the grounds.

For poorer women there were still pills available. In 1918 there was a move to ban them but the issue was given great publicity in 1928 in the curious case of a 70-year-old Church of England clergyman who was sentenced to fifteen months' imprisonment for selling abortifacients by mail order. *Birth Control News* said the case highlighted the fact that many people opposed to birth control are not opposed to abortion. It gave the example of a women who stated, 'I cannot use Dr. Stopes method of birth control for it is very wrong', but went on to comment that the reason she had only four children was that the priest gave her something when she was three months gone each time (*Birth Control News*, March 1928). The general moral panic led to the Advertising Association sending a circular to all newspapers asking them to refuse advertisements, although the pills remained on sale until the law was changed in 1968 (*Birth Control News*, June 1929; Hindell and Simms, 1971).

Other people made use of illegal abortionists, who would either use a syringe or insert an instrument of some kind. Probably the best evidence of the frequency of different methods is the study by Parish (1935) of 1,000 abortion cases in 1930–2. Of these, 485 admitted illegal interference and in only 246 cases was Parish sure there was no interference. Two in five used both drugs and a syringe, a quarter used only drugs and a quarter used just a syringe. One in twenty-five used slippery elm bark, which was derived from a tree in North America and expanded when the bark was soaked in water. However, little is known of those women who did not suffer any problems with their abortion.

The BMA published a special report on abortion in 1936 and one of the members of the committee, Aleck Bourne, carried out an abortion on a girl not yet 15 years old pregnant by rape to try and extend the law more formally. Although we know that many others had been carrying out abortions on wide grounds there seems to have been some confusion. In 1927, Binnie Dunlop published a letter in the *BMJ* saying that abortion after rape was legal (12 November). Yet, while he was saying this and some were carrying out abortion on request, others agreed with the authors of the Birkett Report that 'Technically the procuring of abortion was not permissible in any circumstances whatsoever' (1939, p.39). To those with this view the 1929 Infant Life Preservation Act was important. The aim of this Act was to close a loophole in English law that it was not an offence to kill a child in the process of being born. The Act made this an offence except to save the life of the woman after twenty-eight weeks of pregnancy. After a few years people began to argue that the logic of the Act meant that it was legal to perform abortion at any stage of gestation to save the woman's life. So there were wide differences and the Birkett Committee commented that, although it was not the practice to prosecute medical practitioners who induced abortions for serious medical reasons, there were great differences in interpretation. Bourne's abortion was reported to the police. He was tried and acquitted in 1938, and so it became openly accepted that abortion could be carried out for rape, although it was less certain that it could be carried out for such things as foetal abnormality (Francome, 1984a, pp.68–70).

Although the Birkett Committee commented widely on the law, it was primarily appointed in 1937 to investigate the prevalence of abortion and what could be done. On the basis of some figures published by the British Medical Association, the committee estimated that there were 44,000–60,000 illegal abortions a year (Birkett, 1939; BMA, 1936). However, David Glass (1940) argued that 100,000 was nearer the mark and it was his figure that was given the most publicity after the Second World War (Francome, 1984a, pp.70–3).

Abortion after the Second World War

When the servicemen returned home, many people who had had their lives interrupted by the war started their families and there was a large increase in births. But this does not mean there was no demand for abortion, especially amongst those women who had several children quite quickly. A useful source of data about illegal abortion after the war is provided by Moya Woodside who interviewed forty-four inmates at Holloway (woman's) prison who had been convicted of procuring illegal abortions. She found that many of those involved had a very good record of safety, although some were discovered only after they had caused a death. She found the most common method was the Higginson's syringe, which thirty-five of them used, usually inserting soap and water with a disinfectant. She argued that money was not the major factor, but 'compassion and feminine solidarity were strongly motivating factors' (Woodside, 1963).

For poor women in the postwar years abortion could still be a very dangerous business. One death was instrumental in the repeal of capital punishment in Britain. In 1949 a 19-year-old with one child was living in two small rooms with no indoor lavatory. She took pills and when they did not work sought an abortionist. Christie, the man who lived below her, offered to do it for free, strangled her and put the blame on her husband, who was executed for the crime but posthumously pardoned (Kennedy, 1971).

Richer women were much more fortunate. The Bourne trial of 1938 meant that Harley Street could be even more open about its activities than hitherto. In fact, even before the Abortion Act 1967 came into force, there were numerous legal or semi-legal abortions. In 1966, for example, an estimated 5,700 National Health abortions were carried out under what was known as the Bourne amendment. In addition to this, an estimated 15,000 were performed by doctors privately (Potts, Diggory and Peel, 1970). Further abortions were carried out in Scotland, and indeed Scottish law was more liberal than that of England and Wales. As Dugald Baird commented in a letter to abortion campaigner Vera Houghton, no action could be taken against a doctor performing an abortion unless a complaint was made (letter dated 9 March 1964).

There has been some dispute about the number of illegal abortions in the period coming up to the 1967 Act. There were a series of low estimates from C. B. Goodhart (1964, 1969, 1973). In the last article he commented on the estimate of 100,000 illegal abortions a year in the light of the experience of legal abortion:

> The induced abortion rate (legal and illegal) before the law was changed must be highly relevant to prediction of when and where it can be expected to level off afterwards, which will be of considerable social, medical and demographic importance. If it is true that there were about 100,000 criminal abortions a year before 1967, the large increase in legal abortions since then can largely be accounted for by pregnancies now being terminated legally, which formerly would have been the subject of criminal abortions. That being so, the 96,640 legal abortions registered for resident women in 1971 might indicate that now, at last, criminal abortions had been largely eliminated as a result of the Act; and that therefore the legal abortion rate would be expected to level off at not much above that figure. [Goodhart, 1973]

However, he went on to suggest that if there had only been around 15,000 criminal abortions a year, as he had been estimating, there was no reason to suppose that the abortion rate would stabilise at this or any other figure. Goodhart clearly did not anticipate that the abortion rate would in fact stabilise at just over 100,000. This levelling was one factor amongst many that led me to argue that this figure, although dating back to prewar days, was nevertheless relatively accurate for the 1960s (Francome, 1977).

In conclusion, this chapter indicates that, despite its being illegal prior to 1967, abortion was commonly practised and that the highest level of demand occurred in the period preceding the First World War.

3 The Development of Abortion Practice in the United States

Nineteenth-century abortion practice

At the beginning of the nineteenth-century, English common law applied in the United States, which meant that abortion could be carried out until quickening. There was no nationwide equivalent of the British 1803 Act, so when in 1812 a man named Bangs was charged with administering an abortifacient potion the Massachusetts Supreme Court freed him. It said the indictment did not specify that the woman was quick with child. This case (Commonwealth v Bangs) became a precedent in the United States and was quoted in various other trials during the nineteenth century, including one in 1880 (Mohr, 1978, pp.5, 265).

In 1821, Connecticut became the first state to pass abortion legislation. This made abortion illegal after the woman was quick with child but left it legal in the early part of pregnancy. The first state to introduce a prohibition on abortion without specifying that the woman should be quick with child was in New York in 1828. It barred abortion by 'any medicine, drug, substance or thing whatever, or . . . any instrument or other means whatever, with intent thereby to procure the miscarriage of any such woman, unless the same shall have been necessary to preserve the life of such woman' (Mohr, 1978, p.27). It specified a maximum sentence of one year's imprisonment or a £500 fine.

In the discussion of the introduction of laws against abortion in Britain we saw that one factor was the danger of the operation. This seems to have been the case in New York, and Cyril Means (1970) has argued this case the most clearly. He points out, for example, that at the time the New York law was passed there was great concern at the death rate from all operations and he quoted a contemporary observer as being concerned about 'The rashness of many young practitioners in performing the most important surgical operations for the mere purpose of distinguishing themselves . . . We are advised by old and experienced surgeons, that the loss of life occasioned by the practice is alarming' (Means, 1970, p.138). He went on to argue that only one of the nineteenth-century anti-abortion statutes had judicial construction by a contemporary court explaining why it had been passed, which was the Supreme Court of New Jersey. He said this made it clear that the design of the statute was not so much to prevent the procuring of abortions but rather to guard the health and life of the woman against the consequence of such attempts.

The fact that New York passed such a law does not seem to have led to a rush by other states to introduce their own legislation. In fact, by 1840 sixteen of the twenty-six states still had not passed their own laws. Five had a law dealing only with women quick with child and only five had a law banning abortions throughout the pregnancy, and even in these it was difficult to make any prosecutions because of the difficulty of proving pregnancy.

The lack of prosecutions meant abortion was less in the public view than later, but such evidence as is available suggests that the greatest demand was from single women. For example in a series of public lectures in 1839, the well-known anti-abortionist Professor Hugh Hodge said that most abortions were designed 'to destroy the fruit of illicit pleasure, under the vain hope of preserving reputation by this unnatural and guilty sacrifice' (Hodge, 1854).

In the 1840s it seems that there was a great increase in the number of abortions and that this increase was maintained past the 1870s. Mohr commented:

> As a reasonable guess abortion rates in the United States may have risen from an order of magnitude approximating one abortion for every twenty-five or thirty live births during the first three decades of the nineteenth century to an order of magnitude possibly as high as one abortion for every five or six live births by the 1850's and 1860's. (1978, p.50).

Hale (1860) published an estimate that one in five pregnancies ended in abortion and that nine out of ten married women had attempted one. He said that in his own area of Chicago he had met women who had more than ten children and the same number of abortions.

Apart from the increase in numbers, observers suggest that the nature of those seeking abortions changed so that it became largely married women who had them. Statistical evidence on the number of births seems to support the notion that abortion increased. In 1800, the average American woman bore seven children. There was a slight decline in births during the first three decades but between 1840 and 1850 there was the largest drop of the century. This was the very time that abortion came to public notice and services were openly advertised. By the end of the century the number of births had halved to 3.6 per woman (Mohr, 1978, p.82).

In the mid nineteenth century there were several different channels through which to attempt to get an abortion. Some women used abortifacient pills. The best-known abortionist was a woman calling herself Madame Restell. She used aggressive marketing techniques to get customers and if the pills did not work she organised abortions by other means. Madame Restell's advertisements were relatively obscure but some advertisers made the functions of the pills clear in a way that did not happen in Britain. For example, on 4 January 1845 the *Boston Daily Times* carried an advertisement for Dr Peter's French Renovating Pills which stated that 'although very mild and prompt in their operation, pregnant females should not use them, as they invariably produce a miscarriage' (Mohr, 1978, p.53).

It appears that women usually tried drugs first and turned to other methods if these did not work. A Dr Sunot developed a primitive suction system which consisted of an airtight cup from which the air could be removed and used on the 'lower body' to restore bleeding. Another method was to use electricity. Two long leads were hooked up to a galvanic battery. One end was attached to the lower back and the other 'on the abdomen just over the pubia; but at other times it is necessary to apply it more or less internally' (Hollick, 1849). Sometimes these methods could be used by regular medical practitioners, but at other times by local abortionists. Hale used an intrauterine douching method and argued that abortion was safer the earlier it was performed.

Professor Hodge seems to have been at something of a loss to understand how women, whom he seemed to idealise, could nevertheless seek out abortions. In his book *Criminal Abortion* (1854), he spoke of a woman as 'A being so wonderfully constructed, so beautiful, so interesting, so moral, so intellectual, and so influential for good over the best interests of man, and over the destinies of nations' (p.8).

> We blush while we record the fact, that in this country, in our cities and towns, in this city, where literature, science, morality, and Christianity are supposed to have so much influence; where all the domestic and social virtues are reported as being in full and delightful exercise; even here individuals, male and female, exist, who are continually imbracing their hands and consciences in the blood of unborn infants . . . When such individuals are informed of the nature of the transaction, there is an expression of real or pretended surprise that anyone should deem the act improper . . . Educated, refined and fashionable women – yea in many instances, women whose moral character is, in other respects, without reproach; mothers who are devoted, with an ardent and self denying affection, to the children who already constitute their family, are perfectly indifferent respecting the fetus in utero. They do not seem to realise that the being within them is indeed animate. [Hodge, 1854, pp.17, 18]

Three years after this book was published, a committee was appointed by the Suffolk County Medical Association under the leadership of Horatio Robinson Storer to investigate the subject of criminal abortion with a view to its general suppression. The committee reported in 1859 that abortion was frequent among all classes of society. It gave three reasons for abortion's extensive occurrence. First it stressed the widespread ignorance of the true character of the crime because mothers did not believe the foetus was alive until after quickening. This of course was the same point that Hodge had made. Secondly, it said doctors did not concern themselves with foetal life, and thirdly it drew attention to the 'defects of our laws, both common and statute, as regards the independent and actual existence of the child before birth as a living being' (*Transactions of the American Medical Association*, 1859, p.75). In a separate article, Storer drew attention to the discrepancies between the laws more fully. For example,

> In some of the States, the offence is considered a trifling one, except as affecting the person or life of the mother; this is the case in New Hampshire, Vermont, and Massachusetts . . . In but few instances is the crime, intrinsically considered, accounted a heinous one, and recognised in its true character – an attempt to destroy the life of the child . . . In Ohio [abortion] is called a high misdemeanour; in New York, Michigan, Oregon, Arkansas, and Mississippi, it is styled manslaughter in the first degree. The punishment inflicted in the latter of these States, however, is ridiculously trivial, and in all of them proof of quickening is required'. [*North American Medico-Chirurgical Review*, September 1859].

From 1860 onwards the medical profession was able to persuade many states to change their laws, and between 1860 and 1880 at least forty anti-abortion statutes were passed (Mohr, 1978, p.200).

The high abortion rate at mid-century led to the regular physicians setting up an anti-abortion campaign under Storer's leadership. Storer believed abortion was dangerous and in his book *Why not? A Book for Every Woman* (1866), issued under the order of the American Medical Association, he commented: 'I propose to show that induced abortions . . . are so dangerous to the woman's health, her own physical and domestic best interests, that the induction permitted, or solicitation by one cognisant of their true character, should almost be looked upon as proof of actual insanity' (p.15). He also quoted a series of abortion cases reported by Tardieu where of thirty-four abortions carried out by non-physicians there were twenty-two deaths, whereas in a further fifteen cases by physicians there was not one fatality. So overall nearly half the abortions ended in death. This series of Tardieu was continually referred to in the nineteenth and early twentieth centuries to show the dangers of abortion. In fact, as late as 1932 Parry felt the need to state that Tardieu had had an unusual series. This kind of propaganda would, however, have little effect on a population who would have intimate knowledge of friends and acquaintances who had successfully procured abortions.

In the 1860s the British medical press began to comment on the high US abortion rate. In May 1863, for example, the *British Medical Journal* carried an article in which it quoted the *American Medical Times*:

> Whoever examines the advertising columns of country papers, and marks the large number of nostrums which in various and cunning phrases are recommended as certain to effect abortion, cannot doubt the wide and almost universal prevalence of this crime. It is painful to believe that the public conscience is not alive to the moral turpitude of abortion. It cannot be denied that in every grade of society lax opinions of the criminality of procured abortion exist. It is not alone the ignorant and vicious that consider it no crime; the religious equally entertain the belief that abortions may be practised without a shadow of guilt. Every physician must have been approached by persons of upright motives with solicitations to prescribe remedies or employ means which would terminate an early pregnancy.

The New York Times campaign

The British agitation against abortion seems to have had repercussions in the United States. On 3 November 1870 the *New York Times* (*NYT*) introduced an editorial: 'Margaret Waters, the baby farmer, was executed on Tuesday. London Paper'. It went on to congratulate the British authorities and argued that there were similar practices in New York:

> If anyone doubts that fact let him [sic] turn to the advertising columns of the lower class of Sunday newspapers. Even the pages of certain morning dailies are not free from the occasional taint of hideous traffic. It flaunts in open day, and finds a location in every quarter of this great city. From a 'palatial mansion' in Fifth Avenue down to wretched chambers in the slums of Chatham Street, there is accommodation for the perpetuation of infant murder suited to

every rank and condition of life . . . Nor is the Arcadian simplicity of the country at all free from participation in infanticide. In the rural districts of this State there are quiet unpretending cottages, which seem, amid embowering foliage, the chosen abode of innocence and peace; but from these places wasted baby forms are carried into nameless graves. The 'offence is rank and smells to heaven', why is there no hint of its punishment?

The article argued that respectable citizens had ceased to express indignation because they felt powerless but that it was time for people to rouse themselves.

This opening sally heralded a year-long campaign by the *NYT* to get abortion stopped. As in Britain, there were some brief derogatory allusions to adoption and infanticide, but its main focus was abortion. The *NYT* followed the same techniques as used by the *BMJ* investigators of following up advertisements and exposing the results. It directed its ire particularly at the professional abortionists who had false medical qualifications: one, for example, took the certificate of a deceased doctor, erased his name, inserted his own and placed it in a prominent place. The *NYT* argued that such people, including those who purchased certificates from dubious schools, proceeded to make vast fortunes despite killing many pregnant women along the way. One such case it reported was of a Dr Wolf. When he received a seven-year sentence the *Times* said it 'created a lively feeling of gratification on account of the terrible warning which it gave to the professional abortionists . . . who have hitherto escaped punishment' (*NYT*, 27 January 1871).

The campaign did not have much effect on the number of abortions, however, and seven months later, under the title 'The Evil of the Age', the *NYT* once more reported on the large number: 'Could even a proportion of the facts that have been detected in frightful profusion, by the agents of the Times, be revealed in print, in their hideous truth, the reader would shrink for the appalling picture' (*NYT*, 23 August 1871).

Just four days after this a curious case occurred. The body of a naked 18-year-old woman was found in a trunk due to be sent to Chicago. At first the death was shrouded in mystery. There was no immediate clue to her identity and there were no marks on her body except for decomposition about the pelvic region. This led the *NYT* to comment: 'It was apparent that here was a new victim of man's lust, and the life destroying arts of those abortionists, whose practices have lately been exposed by the Times' (*NYT*, 27 August). The report commented somewhat salaciously that the woman was finely built, had beautiful golden hair and was gazed upon by hundreds of the curious before being taken away. On 30 August, the *Times* announced that the premises of a Dr Rosenzweig had been searched and items of bloody clothing suggested that he was the perpetrator of the abortion.

The campaign by the *New York Times* did get the advertisements to disappear for a while, but by 30 January 1872 it had to admit they had returned. It was in fact not the *Times* but Anthony Comstock who had the greatest effect on the provision of abortion (Francome, 1984a, pp. 46–8). In 1873 he persuaded Congress to pass an Act that made it an offence to sell, offer or give away any article or medicine 'for causing abortion, except on the prescription of a physican in good standing'; it also banned the advertisement and sale of birth control appliances. Comstock used this law to attack abortion with energy and determination. The *Second Annual Report* of the Society for the Suppression of Vice (1876) said that forty-nine abortionists had been arrested, of whom thirty-nine had been convicted and sentenced. In 1878, Comstock finally succeeded in arresting Madame Restell after buying abortifacient preparations from her. The day before her trial she committed suicide (*NYT*, 2 April 1878).

It appears that as a result of Comstock's work most abortifacient advertisements disappeared. Mohr suggests that abortionists usually turned to the use of private cards and handbills and that those advertisements that did appear were more veiled than they had been earlier (1978, p.199). However, Comstock's success was by no means total. In 1888 Pomeroy commented that the law was a 'dead letter', that abortion flourished in the highest places, and that the medical profession not engaged in the practice was silent. He talked of other countries referring to abortion as 'the American sin' and of advertisements that stated 'Married Ladies who have any reason to believe themselves pregnant are particularly cautioned against using these pills *as they will cause a miscarriage*' (pp.56, 64). In 1896 abortion was sufficiently visible for the *Boston Medical and Surgical Journal* to carry an article trying to discover why it should be so common. On the subject of advertisements the paper commented: 'Should we allow the lawless liberty of advertising in our daily papers to remain a source of danger to the innocent and uninstructed' (p.541).

Table 3.1   Number of children under 5 per 1,000 women of childbearing age in the United States

1850	626	1880	559
1860	634	1890	485
1870	572	1900	479

Source: Ross (1907), p.608.

A survey of the birthrates of fourteen European countries over the period 1880–1900 puts the United States data in an international perspective (Ross, 1907). It showed that all the countries had a decline in rates but that the biggest was for England and Wales, followed by Scotland, Hungary and Holland. During the four years 1896–1900, France had the lowest overall birthrate. The changes in the US birthrate from 1850 could be monitored by recording the number of children under 5 years old to every 1,000 women of childbearing age (see Table 3.1). The results showed a decline over each decade but that the drops were much bigger during the decades 1860–70 and 1880–90. Overall, the number of children under 5 dropped by nearly a quarter over the half-century. The reason for the reduction in birthrates is not clear. Ross mentioned that with the emancipation of women men were more likely to take the woman's birth pangs into account, that with the decline in religion few held with Luther that 'God makes children and he will provide for them', and that the increase in education and the abolition of child labour meant children were more expensive to keep. As for the means of the reduction, he said:

The desire to prevent conception has become dominant among women of the great middle class of this country, and in my own medical experience, which lasted only four years, I met hardly a single middle class family in which this was not general, often before the first child was born, and invariably practised after the coming of the first born' [1907, p.629]

Although Ross did not mention it, abortion must have been a further factor in this overall reduction.

Abortion in the United States in the early twentieth century

Comstock's legislation was one factor in two significant differences between the situation in Britain and the United States. The first difference was that birth control came under vigorous attack in the United States. Prior to Comstock's campaign, some birth control information had been available. Dr Knowlton's pamphlet 'The Fruits of Philosophy', discussed in the context of birth control in Britain, was initially published in the United States (in 1832) and it seems that a degree of acceptance had occurred. The *Medical and Surgical Reporter* carried a series of articles in 1888 in which Thomas Pope reported that birth control was a subject that came up almost daily before every physician. He suggested that birth control would lessen the death rate of both mothers and children and argued that there was no danger from the condom. He drew attention to another doctor's view of withdrawal: 'the sexual act is not completed but the emission takes place, consequently he doubted whether this method was attended with any injurous effect' (p.525). Others gave explicit instructions on methods. D. E. Matteson, for example, described withdrawal, the condom, syringe with astringent, and recommended a silk sponge $1\frac{1}{2}''$ in diameter with thread, which was moistened before insertion (p.759). At first Comstock was busy with abortion, pornography and gambling, and did nothing to prosecute this journal. However, in 1907 Robinson – the United States' foremost birth control activist at the time – reported Comstock had begun to prosecute sellers of condoms and, although Robinson was abusive to Comstock and called him 'a stupid ignoramus utterly devoid of all sense and judgement', he was not willing to run his gauntlet by publishing birth control methods and challenging the law (Francome, 1984a, pp.48–51). So birth control was much more an underground activity than it was in Britain.

A second major difference was a change in abortion operators. The attack on abortion advertisements, combined with the exception written into the Comstock law about abortions being carried out by physicians of good standing, led to the suppression of unqualified operators and tilted the balance in the United States towards illegal abortions being performed by doctors.

As a result, it seems that doctors were continuously being asked to carry out abortions. One source of the demand for abortions is indicated in an article entitled 'Remarks on contraception' (1906) by L. Jacobi, an eminent New York doctor. At this time there was no cure for syphilis and Jacobi said it was no good telling a woman 'You must not become pregnant' without instructing her any further. 'A few months later she came to us pregnant, of course, and we then decide to empty her uterus, endangering her life, aggravating her disease and leaving her precisely in the same situation in regard to future conception' (*Medico-Pharmaceutical Critic and Guide*, 1906, p.75). But this was not of course the major source of demand for abortion. In January 1907 the *Critic and Guide* published an article directed towards new medical graduates in which Robinson pointed out that very early in their careers they would be asked to carry out abortions. He commented: 'An abortionist who is aseptic and not too clumsy, can enjoy a lucrative practice, with very few deaths and the man who refuses to perform abortions will lose a good deal of practice and will make enemies of many influential persons.' Robinson none the less suggested that they should make up their minds not to do them.

There were various estimates of the number of abortions in the early twentieth century. A Dr Hunter of Louisville reported calculations, based on correspondence with nearly 100 doctors, that in the United States there were over 100,000 abortions and 6,000 deaths from abortion each year (*Medical Age*, March 1906).

A major work on abortion – and one American academics seem to have missed – was the book published by Taussig, a lecturer in gynaecology at Washington University in 1910. He reported an analysis of 348 women who had been pregnant. Of these, 201 women had had a total of 371 induced and spontaneous abortions. Thirty-six women admitted to instrumental abortion and fifty developed some disease afterwards. Taussig suggested that half of all the abortions were induced but that 'It is always difficult to obtain a confession of such a criminal act from a patient' (p.5). Taussig commented on criminal abortion: 'It may, indeed, be said that it is the one crime that is almost universal, is found among all classes, in all countries.' He talked of press advertisements for abortifacients, and of physicians and midwives who will help women in trouble. He believed abortion was increasing because the discovery of antiseptics had meant that it could be done with less risk of blood poisoning than formerly. Overall he estimated 80,000 criminal abortions each year in New York and 6,000–10,000 in Chicago.

William Robinson stated in 1909 that the numbers of abortions were very high and commented 'When the good moral, Christian people of our land look upon the maiden "who loves not wisely but too well" with more charity and pity . . . then will the evils of abortion rapidly decline . . . let us recognise that bearing a child out of wedlock is not incompatible with true repentance and a future of honour and usefulness' (*Critic and Guide*, 1909, p.72).

In 1911, Robinson estimated that anywhere from 10 per cent to 25 per cent of doctors performed abortions habitually, commenting:

> But I would not blame the profession very strongly for this. It is the State that is to blame for this state of affairs . . . . The laymen have no idea of the frequency of the demand and of the tremendous pressure that is brought to bear upon the medical profession. I venture to say that for every abortion performed by a physician at least one hundred demands, requests and pleading supplications are refused. If this were not so we would not have the thousands and thousands of non medical male and female abortionists, who thrive

throughout this country. A million abortions at a very conservative estimate are performed annually in the United States [*Critic and Guide*, 1911, p.209].

In fact this estimate was well below that of 2 million a year that some doctors had estimated in the 1890s (Gordon, 1977, p.53).

By 1917 Robinson had revised his estimate of medical involvement and argued that 75 per cent of the profession performed abortions at some time if not on a regular basis. He said that he could talk freely on the subject because he was one of the minority (*Critic and Guide*, 1917, p.47).

Robinson was also the first consistent activist for legalised abortion. From 1913 he called for it to be legalised in the early months of pregnancy. Others followed his lead. Dekker argued in 1920 that if abortion were legalised it would reduce the reverse Darwinism by which the poorer groups were over-producing themselves (Francome, 1984a, p.75). A woman's group was formed in 1932 called the Association for the Reformation of the Abortion Law and in 1933 Dr Rongy published *Abortion: Legal or Illegal*.

Margaret Sanger, the birth control campaigner, was at first publicly in favour of abortion. In the pamphlet *Family Limitation* (1915) she argued that there were times when an abortion was justifiable and that women seeking it should do so without delay, although she also argued that abortion would become unnecessary with contraception. Her British advisers were not pleased with her approach as they were concerned she would damage her credibility in the fight for birth control. However, she told them that she was not advocating abortion but just recognising that the practice was so common in the United States that if women had decided to obtain one it was safer to do so as soon as possible (Francome, 1984a, pp.60–2).

The inter-war years

It seems likely that abortion was more common in the United States after the First World War than before it, although estimates varied widely and by their very nature are impossible to verify. An unsigned article in the *Critic and Guide* for 1920 (p.61) reported a survey of doctors known to have performed abortions. From this it was estimated that there were 550,000 abortions a year in the United States taking into account the different patterns in the rural districts. One doctor reported 18,000 abortions at $50 each and the author noted that there were virtually no prosecutions and that the public supported its covert practice. By way of illustration he commented: 'When I first saw Dr. C he was driving by in an automobile and somebody referred to him incidentally as the "leading abortionist in town". This was not given as a secret . . . but as a well known fact as if one were to say offhand "There's the Brooklyn Bridge".' In a following article the anonymous author argued that even the few who were convicted rarely served sentences (p.65).

In 1924 Ettie Arout was quoted in the *Critic and Guide* (July) as saying,

> As a result of the suppression of knowledge of prevenception [a term for birth control no longer used], abortions are widespread and probably accepted as necessary. Educated married women told me quite frankly that they had two or more abortions regularly every year, that they experienced no difficulty in securing efficient and economical service in this way.

Margaret Sanger said in her autobiography that ideas of what to do with an unwanted pregnancy were passed from mouth to mouth. She gave examples of herb teas, turpentine, rolling downstairs, inserting slippery elm and knitting needles. She also pointed out that women visited the local operator: 'On Saturday nights I have seen groups of from fifty to one hundred with their shawls over their heads waiting outside the office of the five dollar abortionist' (Sanger, 1938, p.89).

For poor women, the fact that birth control was difficult to get hold of meant that they often had pregnancies very close together at great detriment to their health. The following letter appeared in Sanger's *Birth Control Review* in January 1918:

> I am a poor married woman in great trouble and I'm writing to you for help. I was married in June 1915 and I have two children little boy 21 mon & a girl 4 mon. and I will be only

17 years old this month and Im in the family way again and Im nearly crazy for when my husband finds out that Im going to have another baby he will beat the life out of me. My husband isn't very strong; he had two operations since we were married and cant do no hard work and doent earn much and then theres always trouble; when we havent enough money he goes out and drinks for all that he gets hold of . . . Im sure Im in the family way though my family doctor won't tell me for he doesn't want to tell me. He said I didn't look in the family way but he was laughing, that was two months ago. Im awful worried and don't know where to call for help, I'm sure Im about three months or nearly 3. So won't you be kind enough and tell me or send me something so that I wont have any more. Please do for Im lost if I have one more baby, I'd rather jump in the river it wouldn't be worse . . . I haven't much but I rather starve a couple weeks or months and get enough money to have so I wouldn't have another baby. [p.13]

For such women abortion was often sought out of desperation.

We saw that the big debate about birth control in Britain was in 1877, but in the United States it was still a contentious issue in the 1930s. *Medical World* of December 1932 called birth control premature abortion and commented: 'Nature originated the sexual act for procreation only, and not as a diversion, amusement or business.' Three years later it had changed its mind on the issue but the authorities still instigated sanctions on birth control. On 6 January 1935 the *Brooklyn Eagle* reported that nine books and magazines largely dealing with birth control were banned from entry to the United States. Similarly, on 2 January the *Buffalo Times* (New York) reported that 'Increased power to prosecute persons who send Birth Control propaganda and devices through the mails was asked by the Post Office Department'. In fact, as late as 1935 the *Critic and Guide* reported the president of the Medical Society of New York attacking the advocates of birth control 'who wished to destroy life . . . . It must be a sign of moral insanity that birth control in its widest and vilest application should be so extensively practiced' (p.197). The medical profession did not support contraception until 1937 when it made a decision that its members could supply information to their patients.

The actual number of abortions in the United States in the 1930s is still a matter of some debate. In 1929 Robinson raised his estimate from 2 to 3 million (*Critic and Guide*, p.53). Margaret Sanger suggested the lower figure but commented:

> It is the opinion of competent medical observers during the last twenty five years that there are more criminal abortions in the United States than any other country in the world. The total of abortions, which does not include the number of those brought about by drugs or by instruments used by the pregnant woman herself, has been estimated to top two millions per year. [*New Generation*, April 1935]

Rongy (1933) also estimated 2 million. Isolated examples suggest that these estimates may not have been too high. Recent data indicate that there are currently $1\frac{1}{2}$ million abortions each year in the United States, but the level of birth control and sterilisation use was much lower in the 1930s. In 1933, the *Critic and Guide* gave a couple of examples to show the level of abortion use. It reported that a Dr Kahn had investigated a perforated uterus and was told that the patient had had seven abortions in two years (p.298). Later, the journal told of a married 17 year old who had had four abortions in one year (p.302). It would be almost impossible to find women with so many abortions in the US in the 1980s.

Taussig's major work on abortion is an important source of information (1936). He summarised the laws in the various states into five groups. Abortion was not allowed at all in Florida, Massachusetts, New Jersey, Louisiana, New Hampshire and Pennsylvania. It was allowed in order to save the woman's life in Alabama, Arizona, California, Connecticut, Delaware, Idaho, Illinois, Indiana, Iowa, Kentucky, Maine, Michigan, Minnesota, Montana, Nebraska, Nevada, New York, North Carolina, North Dakota, Oklahoma, Oregon, Rhode Island, South Carolina, South Dakota, Tennessee, Utah, Vermont, Virginia, Washington, West Virginia and Wyoming. It was legal to save the life of the woman if medically advised in Arkansas, Georgia, Kansas, Missouri, Ohio, Texas and Wisconsin. In Colorado, District of Columbia, Maryland and New Mexico it was legal also to safeguard the woman's health and, finally, in Mississippi it was legal when deemed necessary by a physician (1936, p.430).

These laws were, however, largely irrelevant to what was occurring in practice. Taussig quoted the work of Dr Marie Kopp who investigated the records of 10,000 women attending a birth control clinic. Just over half had had abortions and these had a total of 11,172. Out of this overall figure, 3,165 were spontaneous, 340 were therapeutic and 7,677 were deliberate. In all, one in five pregnancies ended in induced abortion (1936, p.368). A study of 991 women at a birth control clinic in New York found a similar level of one abortion for five pregnancies (p.369). The high number of pregnancies was clearly one factor in the great number of abortions. Kopp for example showed that for married women 4 per cent of first pregnancies were aborted, compared to 28 per cent of fourth ones and 48 per cent of the ninth or higher pregnancies (p.371).

In 1942 Alan Guttmacher called on the medical profession to relax its barriers on abortion and quoted the New York prosecutor that there were 100,000–250,000 criminal abortions each year in the city (*New York Times*, 31 January 1942).

Abortion after the Second World War

The estimates of the number of abortions in the postwar years seem much lower than in the inter-war period. Planned Parenthood organised a conference on abortion in 1957. From the evidence presented at this conference, Calderone suggested: 'A plausible estimate of the frequency of induced abortion in the United States could be as low as 200,000 and as high as 1,200,000 a year' (1958, p.180). In the event, most observers were inclined towards the higher of these two figures and the figure of 1 million abortions a year was the one most often quoted.

In terms of hospital abortions, Tietze (1983) suggested that these declined somewhat between the 1940s and 1960s. However, he went on to suggest that from that time they began to rise. He pointed out, for example, that in 1964 about 4,000 abortions were carried out because the woman had contracted rubella in the first trimester even though this was not an indication allowed by the laws of any state.

There were also various doctors who carried out abortions in defiance of the law but who tried to be as circumspect as possible. From the mid-1960s onwards, however, there were those who wanted a much more open law and were willing to challenge it. One such was Bill Baird who came out for the right to choose an abortion in the early 1960s. His agitation led to doctors calling him and expressing a willingness to carry out abortions. In a taped interview in 1979 he told me that he set up an underground network. He checked out the doctors and made sure that they·had qualified as an M.D. although he was not worried if they had since lost it. He also watched them carry out a procedure. He usually managed to get the cost down from about $600 to $300 but even at this level the cost of an abortion was about twice the level it would be fifteen years later. He told me that to protect himself he made women sign a statement as follows:

'I came to Bill Baird voluntarily seeking his abortion help. I am not connected to the Police Department. I was charged no fee and I do not hold him responsible for my actions'.

Even so he had some problems. He found out for example that one of the doctors to whom he was sending women was getting them to have sexual intercourse before agreeing to perform the abortion.

Quack abortionists usually carried out their operations in motel rooms. Baird commented:

They used to take two dresser drawers to raise the bed for the right height for the doctor to work. The former medical examiner of New York City – Max Helpern – told me as we stood at public hearings that the quack abortionists took the highest motel room. If he screwed up with the abortion he would push the body out of the window. [Taped interview]

Baird's challenge to the law became increasingly open and in 1967 an American black women's magazine carried on its front page the statement: 'If you want an abortion call 516-538-2626.' In that year too the Clergy Consultation Service was formed and on 27 May the *New York Times* revealed that twenty-one Jewish and Protestant clergymen were going to refer women for abortion (Carmen and Moody, 1973). Activists like these and Maginnis on the West Coast were attacking the law in a manner that had not been seen before (Francome, 1984a, pp.103–11). So by the 1960s abortion had ceased to be as secretive a topic as it had been hitherto.

However, the main feature of this evidence is that, despite legal prohibitions, abortion has been a common operation for well over 100 years. In both Britain and the United States women have sought to end unwanted pregnancies despite the fact that often the risks to their lives and health were very great.

4 *Abortion in Britain since 1967*

This chapter falls into three parts. First there is a brief overview of the official data on the provision of abortion in England and Wales and the main demographic features. However, my main purpose is to set out the results of the survey of a random sample of 649 patients for abortion with a view to considering possible gaps in the service in terms of sex education, birth control and abortion provision, and the needs of the population. A final section deals with provision in Scotland.

Abortion provision in England and Wales since 1967

Number of abortions

The first year of full operation of the Abortion Act was 1969 and Table 4.1 shows the number of abortions on indigenous women in England and Wales in successive years. The data show a steady rise in the number of abortions until 1973. This is presumably in large part due to the transfer of the operation from the illegal to the legal sector and the gradual atrophy of the illegal abortion network as legal services developed. Certainly individual case histories show evidence of this pattern. A 31-year-old woman approached me after I had given a lecture in December 1984 and told me of her experience. When she was young she was 'too embarrassed' to discuss birth control with her boyfriends and in 1971 she became pregnant. She did not know how to get a legal abortion and it did not occur to her to go to her local doctor, so she asked around and was introduced 'to someone who knew someone'. On the designated day she waited on a corner in Bristol and was driven to the address. There she met a woman who had trained as a nurse who gave her the abortion for £5 using a Higginson's

Table 4.1   Abortions and marital status: England and Wales (residents), 1969–1984

| | Number ('000s) | | | |
Year	All	Single	Married	Widowed/ divorced/ separated	Rate per 1,000 women, 15–44
1969	49.8	22.2	23.0	4.6	5.3
1970	76.0	34.5	34.3	7.2	8.1
1971	94.6	44.4	41.5	8.7	10.1
1972	108.6	51.1	46.9	10.6	11.5
1973	110.6	52.9	46.8	10.9	11.5
1974	109.4	53.3	45.2	10.9	11.5
1975	106.2	52.4	43.1	10.7	11.0
1976	101.0	50.5	39.9	10.6	10.4
1977	102.7	52.1	39.9	10.7	10.4
1978	111.9	56.4	42.2	13.3	11.3
1979	120.6	63.1	43.7	13.8	12.0
1980	128.9	68.7	44.3	15.9	12.8
1981	128.6	71.0	43.0	14.6	12.5
1982	128.5	72.9	41.1	14.5	12.3
1983	127.4	74.3	38.9	14.2	11.9
1984	136.4	82.3	39.2	14.8	12.6

Sources: Office of Population Censuses and Surveys (OPCS), Ref AB 84/6; OPCS (1984) p.1; OPCS (1985) p.7; OPCS *Monitor*, Ref AB 85/3 August 1985.
Note: Unknown status distributed in proportion.

syringe. She said this experience taught her a lesson and so she went to a family planning clinic in Bristol and used the pill for a number of years. However, she became a little casual about regular use and became pregnant again. By this time she knew of the possibility of a legal abortion and so she went to her doctor.

There has been some debate over the number of illegal abortions occurring after the 1967 Act (Cavadino, 1976; Francome, 1976b, 1977 and 1984a). However, it now seems clear that there are very few. The number of deaths from illegal abortion fell over this period from forty-seven in 1966 to eight in 1973 and in subsequent years illegal abortion deaths have been virtually unknown.

In 1974, the government introduced free birth control on the

National Health Service (NHS), available irrespective of marital status. This was probably the primary force in the reduction of the abortion rate between 1975 and 1977. Yet there was then a substantial rise in the number of abortions, from 103,000 in 1977 to 129,000 three years later. The reasons for this are not totally clear. The scare about the pill was probably a large factor as many women switched their method of birth control to less efficient forms. A further factor is the age structure. The increase in the proportion of women in their late teens was crucial because their demand for abortion is much higher than the overall average for the age group 15–44. Other less important influences on the overall rate were an increase in the incidence of rubella, leading to abortion for foetal deformity, and possibly the use of English addresses by Irish women seeking abortions in England (see Table 4.5 below).

On the question of age it is instructive to consider the figures for 1984 more closely. The figures in Table 4.2 show that it is the age group 16–19 that has the highest abortion rate. This illustrates the fact that abortion provision prevents young women being forced into having a baby at a time in their lives when they are unable to care for it properly. When their life circumstances improve, they are better able to take on the responsibility, possibly with a different partner.

Table 4.2   Legal abortion by age: England and Wales, 1984

Ages	No. ('000s)	Rate per 1,000 women
under 16	4.2	5.5
16–19	33.4	20.6
20–24	39.1	20.1
25–29	24.3	14.3
30–34	17.2	10.2
35–39	13.3	7.4
40–44	4.4	3.1
45 +	0.4	0.3

Source: OPCS *Monitor*, Ref AB 85/3, August 1985.
Note: The rate for the under-16 age group is based on the population of women aged 14–15 and for the 45+ age group on the population of women aged 45–49. Cases of unknown age are distributed proportionately.

Method of obtaining an abortion

Women in Britain do not have the right to an abortion at any stage of pregnancy, so some initiative is needed on the part of the woman in finding a sympathetic doctor if her own does not follow her wishes or if the local consultants are anti-abortion. Many women therefore face difficult hurdles in procuring an abortion. Some women manage to get their abortions free on the NHS, while others pay for their operations in an approved clinic, of which there are around sixty in England and Wales. To get a free abortion, the woman must normally approach one of the GPs in her own practice. After consultation and confirmation of the pregnancy, if the woman has grounds under the 1967 Abortion Act the doctor will then refer her to a local hospital. Here the consultant will decide whether to accept her for an abortion.

If a woman is refused an NHS abortion she can either approach one of the major charitable clinics or go to the private sector. This can involve great difficulties, especially for poor women or those who are unemployed because the cost is around £130. However, the charities do make some provision for deferred payment or reduced cost for particular cases of hardship.

Regional variations in NHS provision

Whether a woman is given a free abortion or not depends to a large extent in which of the fifteen Regional Health Authorities she lives. The percentage of abortions on the NHS in 1980–3 according to region is shown in Table 4.3. The figures show that almost nine out of ten women in the Northern region had their abortions on the NHS, whereas in the West Midlands the figure is just over one in five – although 3,000 agency abortions were also provided free. In May 1985 one area of the West Midlands started a new scheme of 'low cost' abortions. Instead of using their available money to provide free abortions to a small group of women they subsidised all abortions, so that each woman pays £60. The decrease in the percentage of NHS abortions in Wessex in 1982 was largely due to the fact that the Regional Health Authority made an arrangement with the

Table 4.3   National Health Service abortions as a percentage of total abortions in different regions, 1980–1983 (residents)

Region	1983 %	1982 %	1981 %	1980 %
Northern	87	88	89	88
Yorkshire★	36	37	40	38
Trent	58	55	55	54
East Anglia	79	77	76	75
NW Thames	43	41	40	40
NE Thames	51	51	50	50
SE Thames	51	50	49	48
SW Thames★	38	40	39	36
Wessex★	45	46	52	50
Oxford	52	50	50	51
South-Western	81	78	77	75
West Midlands★	21	21	21	22
Mersey	52	52	30	27
North Western	42	41	42	42
Wales	—	60	59	57

Source: OPCS *Monitor* Refs AB 84/1 and AB 85/5; OPCS (1985), p.32.

★ *Note*: agency agreements in operation.

British Pregnancy Advisory Service (BPAS) that they should carry out the abortions on an agency basis. The abortions would still be free. There was a large increase in NHS provision in Merseyside – from 27 per cent in 1980 to 52 per cent in 1982 – due to the opening of a new day care unit.

Gestation

Table 4.4 shows that more than 85 per cent of abortions on resident women occur under 12 weeks and just over a third occur under 9 weeks. However, this overall figure masks a wide variation between the NHS and the non-NHS sector. Abortions in the non-NHS sector are on average carried out earlier in the pregnancy, more than twice as many non-NHS abortions occurring within the first 9 weeks of gestation. This difference would be even greater if it were not for the fact that some women only go to the private or charitable sector after

Table 4.4 Length of gestation at abortion: Engl.
Wales, 1983 (residents)

Weeks of gestation	Percentage of abortions		
	All premises	NHS	Non-NH.
under 9 weeks	34.5%	22.7%	45.9%
9–12	50.9%	64.5%	38.0%
13–14	6.6%	6.3%	6.8%
15–16	3.5%	3.7%	3.4%
17–18	2.3%	1.6%	3.0%
19–20	1.2%	0.8%	1.6%
21–22	0.5%	0.2%	0.8%
23–24	0.3%	0.1%	0.4%
24 +	0.1%	0.1%	0.05%
unknown	0.1%	0.1%	0.05%

Source: OPCS (1985) p.6.

they have been turned down for an NHS abortion. A survey in
Wessex showed that 16 per cent of patients at the BPAS clinic
had been refused NHS terminations (Ashton, 1978). However,
it is often not a refusal of an NHS abortion that drives women
to the private or charitable sector but rather the degree of
unnecessary bureaucracy to which they would be subjected.
Some women pay for an abortion rather than face pleading
their case with a consultant and having the uncertainty over the
decision, apart from the fact that they may be suffering side-
effects of pregnancy such as morning sickness.

Several reports have been critical of NHS abortion delays. A
study of the Camden area of London in 1981 showed that two-
thirds of women who could afford private treatment had an
early abortion as against only one-half for NHS abortions, and
that patients were often distressed by this:

Going by my GP's reaction, it would take quite a while to
get an NHS one. Nigh impossible. The appointment takes so
long. Everyone here has tried the NHS and been told that
they can't be seen for at least a week. You go to PAB and
you can see them in two days and everyone gets sorted out
quickly. [Clarke, Farrell and Beaumont, 1983]

My own research was not specifically concerned with delays

but some of the respondents made similar comments. A 21-year-old student, for example, said: 'As a student living in London I made every effort to get the pregnancy terminated on the NHS but the attitudes of the doctors and above all the two week waiting list made this too difficult.' Even when account is taken of the fact that the NHS probably getes a higher proportion of those at the ends of the age range who are more likely to present late, there is clearly still a strong need to reduce waiting time.

In 1984, the Royal College of Obstetricians and Gynaecologists (RCOG) published its report *Late Abortions in England and Wales* (Alberman and Dennis, 1984). This expressed concern that, in 1981, 16 per cent of all legal abortions were carried out in the second trimester, and that 2.3 per cent occurred after nineteen weeks. The report identified four phases of delay: recognition of the pregnancy, the decision to seek an abortion, locating and obtaining medical agreement and a clinic or hospital to carry out the operation, and waiting for admission after agreement has been confirmed.

Delay due to non-recognition of pregnancy was present in 11 per cent of cases where abortion occurred under twelve weeks but rose to over 40 per cent where the abortion occurred after the fourteenth week. The major reasons given for this delay were failed contraception and irregular menstruation. Overall there was reported delay in 14 per cent of cases at this stage and 10 per cent of it was due to these two factors. An incorrect pregnancy test was a factor in 1 per cent of those aborted at 12 weeks or less, 1–2 per cent of those having their abortions at 13–19 weeks and 2.5 per cent of those over 20 weeks. The RCOG said its data showed that in only 5 per cent of cases was delay definitely caused by the doctor. One curious omission from the report, however, was criticism of the fact that pregnancy tests in this country take so long to administer. In the United States it is a relatively simple matter for a woman to get a free test performed quite adequately by a nursing assistant with an immediate result. It is therefore something of a mystery why British GPs cannot set up a similar service rather than sending the samples off to the local hospital with the increased possibilities of loss and confusion, apart from the extra time taken. The report of delays at this stage must also be considered as a minimum because the GPs taking part in the survey would take extra care. Discussions I have had with women as part of my research indicate that they believe that doctors sometimes deliberately create delay in the hope the women will continue with their pregnancy.

'I went to my doctor and at first he said I wasn't pregnant. For a month I felt unwell and when I went back to him he said I was three and a half months and that I was too late for an abortion. I believe he said I wasn't pregnant on purpose. I continued with the pregnancy but had a miscarriage.

These kinds of comments are by no means unusual and point to a problem not considered by the RCOG report.

One area that was well covered by the RCOG report was the delay between referral by the first doctor and the final carrying out of the operation. Of those women aborted at 13–14 weeks, 25.6 per cent had been referred by the ninth week, as had 16.8 per cent of those who were aborted at 15–16 weeks. Even more surprising was the fact that over a fifth of the women aborted at 20–23 weeks had been referred at 12 weeks and 7 per cent had been referred at 9 weeks. A Birth Control Trust report gave case histories showing the experiences of different women:

A separated woman, aged 27, went to her GP when her period was one week late. He told her she was too early and to return in four to five weeks. The pregnancy test took ten days by which time she was around twelve weeks pregnant. Her GP then referred her to a consultant but the appointment was delayed because the consultant was on holiday. She was 15 weeks pregnant before she was seen. The consultant agreed to perform the abortion and told her he would admit her for the operation when possible. She waited for the appointment but nothing happened. After a while she phoned the hospital and was told that the doctor was away again. She told the hospital of her concern over the lateness of the pregnancy and was told she was now too late and they could not perform the abortion. By the time she found alternative help she was at least 21 weeks pregnant. [Chambers, 1981]

The RCOG report also found that even after seeing the consultant there was delay in getting an abortion. In less than half the cases of abortion after 14 weeks gestation in the NHS were the operations carried out within one to two weeks of the consultation. So there is clearly a great scope for improvement in services.

We shall see that abortions are much simpler to obtain in the United States and are performed on average much earlier.

Safety of abortion

Peter Diggory caused a stir when he published an article in the *Lancet* (27 October 1984) arguing that over the period 1978–82 legal abortions were eleven times as dangerous on the NHS as in the private sector. In the private sector and charity clinics there were two deaths out of 488,860 abortions (0.4 per 100,000), while in the NHS there were thirteen deaths out of 295,640 abortions (4.4 per 100,000).

In the 3 November 1984 issue of the journal, however, there were various criticisms of Diggory's figures. F. C. Martin pointed out that women originally having a private abortion are often transferred to an NHS hospital when there were problems. Phillip Kestleman made a number of points, including the fact that the NHS was four times as likely to perform an abortion to save the woman's life, that it had a higher percentage of those over the age of 35, and that it was more likely to carry out sterilisation with abortion, which is known to increase the risks. So Diggory's figures must largely be seen as raising a potential problem rather than pointing to a definite difference.

None the less, there are clearly great differences in safety between countries and services. The two British charities that co-operated with this study have excellent records. To the end of 1985 BPAS had carried out 321,389 abortions and Marie Stopes 18,310 without a single death (personal communication). Similarly, Evert Ketting told me (4 February 1986) that the Dutch daycare units outside of hospitals had their last death in 1974 and since that time have performed over 600,000 abortions. These kinds of facts suggest that good medical care could bring the risks of an abortion death almost down to zero.

Abortions on foreign women

No résumé of abortion practice in Britain could be complete without some discussion of the fact that, despite its faults, the British abortion service has been a source of respite for many foreign women over the years. Indeed, as I have argued elsewhere, the British law was very important in bringing legal changes to other countries (Francome, 1984a). The figure for foreign women coming to Britain for abortion are shown in Table 4.5.

Table 4.5   Country of origin of foreign women having their abortions in England and Wales, 1974–1984

Country	1974	1976	1978	1979	1980	1981	1982	1983	1984
Scotland	1,038	925	978	1,020	1,198	998	898	814	781
Northern Ireland	1,102	1,118	1,301	1,429	1,585	1,441	1,510	1,460	1,530
Irish Republic	1,406	1,802	2,533	2,767	3,380	3,603	3,653	3,677	3,946
Belgium*	641	364	341	231	200	153	122	75	52
France	36,541	4,459	3,318	2,964	4,219	4,100	3,825	3,796	3,931
German Federal Republic	6,112	2,376	1,216	726	603	514	365	298	258
Italy	1,730	7,881	4,247	961	802	642	626	617	715
Spain	2,863	6,022	14,082	16,433	18,947	20,454	21,415	22,002	20,060
South Africa	n.a.	n.a.	n.a.	n.a.	n.a.	511	563	560	755

Source: OPCS (1984) p.52; OPCS (1985) p.54; and OPCS *Monitor*, Series AB 1974–80 and August 1985, Ref AB 85/3.
Note: * figures include Luxembourg.

In the early years of the 1967 Act many women came from the United States for abortions. The legalisation in New York in 1970 ended this need. There were, however, increasing numbers of French women, and in 1975 over 36,000 came to Britain. (At the time there were only three times as many indigenous women having abortions.) The French legalisation reduced the number to 3,000 in 1979 and subsequently to around the 4,000 mark. Most of these come because of the very short French time limit. In terms of total numbers, Spanish women continue to predominate and in 1984 constituted nearly two-thirds of the foreign residents having their abortions in Britain. A substantial number also go to Holland for their abortions.

The total number of Irish women travelling to Britain rose to nearly 5,500 in 1984. The bigger percentage increase was from the Republic and the figure of almost 4,000 was an all-time high. The number of Northern Ireland women travelling to Britain for abortions was still below the peak reached in 1980.

In recent years there has been some tendency for South African women to travel to Britain for abortions and in 1984 there was an almost 50 per cent increase in numbers. However, the overall figures make it clear that, as always, it was the women from predominantly Catholic countries who have to travel abroad for their abortions.

The British survey sample

Characteristics of the sample

The aim of the empirical research was to obtain a sample of British and United States women to investigate such factors as birth control practice to identify differences between the countries that could explain the abortion rates. As discussed in the Introduction, an attempt was made to make the sample representative of the different kinds of abortion providers. The British sample therefore included patients in the private and the charitable sectors as well as the NHS. It also included a small number of respondents who received their abortions in Scotland; these are included in the overall figures except in the final section where they are separated out. This was the first attempt to carry out such a survey in Britain and it is instructive to consider how the sample compares in certain demographic features with the total abortion patients for England and Wales for 1983 – the year when the bulk of the questionnaires were collected.

Table 4.6 compares the age structure of the sample with that of national data. It shows that my sample was broadly representative of the total population. However, it did seem slightly to under-represent the higher and lower ages and over-represent the age group 20–24. This was possibly because the sample slightly under-represented patients having their abor-

Table 4.6 Comparison of age structure of survey sample with national data

Age	No.	Survey sample %	England & Wales (1983) %
under 19	164	25.3	27.7
20–24	215	33.1	27.5
25–34	188	28.9	30.7
35 +	64	9.9	14.0
not known	18	2.8	0.1
Total	649	100.0	100.0

Sources: OPCS (1985) p.4 and this survey.
Note: Sample data include Scottish results.

Table 4.7 Comparison of marital status of survey sample with national data

Status	Survey sample No.	%	England and Wales (1983)
Married	165	25.4	30.2
single	399	61.5	57.5
widowed/divorced/ separated	73	11.3	11.0
not known	12	1.8	1.3
Total	649	100.0	100.0

Source: OPCS (1985) p.7 and this survey.

tions on the NHS, who are disproportionately the 'hard cases' – either past normal childbearing age or very young.

Comparison can also be made of the marital status of my sample with the overall population. Table 4.7 shows that the sample was slightly under-represented in terms of the married and the widowed, divorced and separated, with a consequent slight over-representation of the single in comparison with the national data for England and Wales. However, the differences were not great.

There is a cultural difference between Britain and the United States over asking questions about race and religion. In Britain, race was left out of the 1981 census because a satisfactory question could not be devised that would be acceptable to all the groups involved. In the United States, questions about race are acceptable but questions about religion are not, whereas these are acceptable in Britain. In my questionnaire I asked people, 'In which of the following racial groups would you place yourself?' A list was given and the results were as shown in Table 4.8. The sample contained a total of 53 women (8.5 per cent) from the two main non-white groups in Britain. As no official data are collected it is not possible to gauge accurately whether any of the ethnic groups are over-represented. However, it seems that they are present more or less in proportion to their population estimates in the groups of childbearing age. The vast majority of women abortion patients were white and only 1.6 per cent were Hispanic, oriental or of other racial group.

Respondents' replies to a question about religious preference are shown in Table 4.9. The data showed that 54.3 per cent identified wtih one of the Protestant groups. Fully three in ten did not respond or had no religion they were willing to report. This is higher than other comparable surveys and may be due to the wording of my question, which could mean that people brought up in a religion but no longer practising would say they had no current religious practice. In all, 12.8 per cent of the sample said they were Catholic, which is only slightly higher than the 11.8 per cent Catholics reported in a survey carried out by Gallup in 1982 (Francome, 1982). So Catholics

Table 4.8 Racial characteristics of survey sample

Grouping	No.	%
black	25	3.8
white	569	87.7
Asian	28	4.3
Hispanic	4	0.6
other	5	0.8
Oriental	1	0.2
not known	17	2.6
Total	649	100.0

Table 4.9   Religious characteristics of survey sample

Religion	No.	%
Catholic	83	12.8
Protestant	352	54.3
Jewish	3	0.5
Muslim/Hindu	17	2.6
not known/none	194	29.8
Total	649	100.0

in Britain do not seem over-represented in terms of the number of abortions.

In all, the data show that my sample corresponds relatively well to the national profile of abortion patients.

Results of the survey

Sex education   After the classificatory questions, the survey set out to discover something of the nature of sex education in a non-threatening way by asking the women the source of their first knowledge about menstruation. They were asked 'When you had your first menstrual period, had anyone told you what to expect? If so, who?' The replies are given in Table 4.10. Just over half the total sample stated that they had received the first information about their periods from their mothers. If the 8.0 per cent who did not respond to the question are redistributed in proportion then the number receiving their first information from their mother rose to nearly 60 per cent. The division in parental roles is quite clear. Only two of the fathers were the first source of information and if the mother was deceased the job was often left to another female relative such as a grandmother.

The degree of the sex division may be of some surprise but of concern is the fact that one respondent in four (24.6 per cent) had no prior knowledge about menstruation. I carried out interviews to investigate the problem further. One 33-year-old woman said she had not known what to expect. She began her periods at the age of 10 and told me: 'I was brought up by my Dad and brother and they did not say anything about it. When I started to bleed I was really frightened and went to see the

Table 4.10   Source of first information about menstruation

Source	No.	%	Corrected %
mother	353	54.4	59.1
father	2	0.3	0.3
friend	21	3.2	3.5
teacher	50	7.7	8.4
sibling	15	2.3	2.5
relative	7	1.1	1.2
doctor	2	0.3	0.3
no one	147	22.7	24.6
not known	52	8.0	
Total	649	100.0	100.0

Table 4.11   Age at commencement of periods

Age	No.	%
under 11	12	1.8
11	91	14.0
12	147	22.7
13	166	25.6
14	132	20.3
15	70	10.8
16	21	3.2
17	4	0.6
not known	6	0.9
Total	649	100.0

woman over the road. I've made sure my 10-year-old daughter knows all about it.' Another said she had read about menstruation from adverts and had heard something at school but was surprised: 'I was in the bathroom and I started to bleed so I thought I'd cut myself.'

One reason for the lack of knowledge may be because the family and school are not adequately prepared for the early onset of menstruation. The data in Table 4.11 show that nearly two-thirds of my sample had had their first period before they were 14 and that only one in twenty-five had to wait until their sixteenth birthday. The reduction in age of puberty obviously

Table 4.12   Age at first intercourse

Age	No.	%	Corrected %
15 or under	74	11.3	11.8
16–17	269	41.4	43.0
18–19	186	28.7	29.7
20–24	85	13.1	13.6
25–29	7	1.1	1.1
30–34	3	0.5	0.5
35–39	2	0.3	0.3
not known	23	3.5	
Total	649	100.0	100.0

has strong implications for the need for early sex education in school, even if it is of a simple nature to make the basic information of bodily functions known. One in six of the sample had their first period at the age of 11 or under and some of these were still at junior school. So a sizeable minority will be at the risk of not being informed unless there is some rudimentary sex education by the age of 9.

First intercourse   There is some evidence that the age at first sexual intercourse is falling and this is discussed later in the chapter (p.84). For my British sample, Table 4.12 shows that 11.3 per cent had their first intercourse below the minimum legal age, and over half the sample had had had their first intercourse below the age of 18. The women's partners seemed somewhat older, as Table 4.13 shows. This tends to confirm the assertion I made in the introduction that women tend to start their sexual experience with older partners and that in general female sexual behaviour occurs at an earlier age than it does for men. The data show that only 2.5 per cent of the partners were under the age of 16, which is less than a quarter of the comparable figure for the women.

Another interesting question is the relationship of the woman to her first partner at first intercourse. Respondents were given a checklist of 'casual boyfriend', 'steady boyfriend', 'husband to be', or 'other', and the results are tabulated in Table 4.14. The data show that in three-fifths of the cases the first intercourse was with a steady boyfriend. The second

Table 4.13 Partner's age at woman's first intercourse

Age	No.	%
14–15	16	2.5
16–17	116	17.9
18–19	168	25.9
20–24	229	35.3
25–29	63	9.7
30–34	20	3.1
35–39	6	0.9
40 +	17	2.6
not known	14	2.1
Total	649	100.0

Table 4:14 Relationship with partner at first intercourse

Relationship	No.	%
casual	88	13.6
steady	391	60.2
fiancé/husband to be	111	17.1
other	10	1.5
husband	31	4.8
not known	18	2.8
Total	649	100.0

biggest category was that of 'husband to be' and in this group is included any who replied 'fiancé'. Just over one in eight said they had their first intercourse with a casual friend. The questionnaire deliberately did not have a separate category for 'husband' as I did not want respondents to feel the researcher might be censorious of any premarital behaviour. However, it was possible for the women to make it clear that it was her husband by simply ringing just 'husband' or by writing it in. In the sample as a whole there were 238 women who were either currently married or had been married at some time. Of these, thirty-one stated their first intercourse was with their husband, which is just under one woman in seven. So there was little

Table 4.15   Birth control use at first intercourse

Method	Sample survey No.	%	United Kingdom (1983) %
pill	135	20.8	27
IUD	3	0.5	8
cap (diaphragm)	12	1.8	1
sheath	195	30.0	15
withdrawal	104	16.0	} 5
safe period	26	4.0	
suppositories	3	0.5	–
foam	4	0.6	–
not using/not known	167	25.8	22
sterilisation	—	—	22
Total	649	100.0	100 (n = 1,100)

Source: Family Planning Information Service (1984a) and this survey.

evidence of chastity except within the Asian community and to a lesser extent amongst the Scottish women (see below).

Birth control at the early stages of intercourse   Earlier research by Joan Lambert (1971) had suggested that birth control was less likely to be used in the early acts of intercourse than later in the relationship. Respondents were therefore asked 'Did you or your partner use any method of birth control? If so what method?' They were then presented with a checklist. The replies are given in Table 4.15. For comparative purposes the table also gives data on birth control usage of a national sample of fertile women in the United Kingdom (Great Britain and Northern Ireland) for part of the period of the study (1983). This survey was conducted by Taylor Nelson Medical, a market research agency specialising in the field (Family Planning Information Service, 1984a). The data show that the most popular method of birth control at first intercourse was the condom, which was used in three cases out of ten. Only one in five couples used the pill, presumably because first intercourse is not often planned sufficiently far ahead for appointments to be made and the pills to take effect.

One in six couples where the woman was having intercourse for the first time used the withdrawal method. Overall, nearly half used male methods of birth control, just over a quarter used female methods, and a similar percentage used nothing or did not reply.

The first experience of sexual intercourse is a significant event in most people's lives. Sometimes it is carefully planned. For example, an 18-year-old London female told me:

> We had been planning it for a while and knew that his parents were going away for the weekend and he was to have a party. We were to sleep in his parents' double bed in honour of the occasion. He bought the things [condoms] and we read the instructions together to make sure we got it right.

However, on other occasions it occurs by 'surprise'. A 21-year-old Northern schoolteacher told me of her experience four years earlier.

> I had been going out with this rugby player for a few months and things had been going further and further. Then one Saturday night we went to a party and I was surprised to find we ended up staying the night. As to birth control I never even thought of it.

Traditionally it was always the boy who played the assertive role in pressing for sexual behaviour. The idea was that he had a strong sexual drive and the girl had to control the situation. Typical advice from a booklet for teenagers entitled *Your Jackie Dating Guide* cautioned young teenagers as follows: 'Do be the one who sets the pace – it's easier for the girl and less embarrassing than trying to call a halt when you've let things go too far' (Francome, 1976a). Although there have clearly been many changes in the patterns of relationships, the evidence of my previous research into teenagers suggests that with the liberalisation of sexual attitudes the basic patterns of relationship have not changed, but there has been a loosening of the norms (Francome, 1976c, 1984a). The double standard still exists but it is no longer frowned upon for a woman to have intercourse before marriage. Young women nowadays may be criticised for too casual an attitude towards sexuality but there are many fewer occasions when teenagers talk of 'saving themselves' for marriage in the way that occurred in some circumstances in the 1950s.

The fact that young men still take an assertive role underlines the overall importance for male responsibility in early birth control. Male methods of contraception are easily available in shops, chemists and public houses. They are also available in the evenings and without medical prescription so there is no need for more than rudimentary planning. My results are therefore of little surprise as they show the popularity of male methods of birth control at first intercourse. Further implications of this finding will be discussed later, but it is clear that any educational programme aiming to reduce teenage pregnancy needs to take male responsibility into account.

The data on birth control practice among the FPIS sample reveal a very different situation. For example, sterilisation did not figure in my study, whereas it occurred amongst over one in five of the national sample, with the numbers dividing fairly evenly between vasectomies and female sterilisation (FPIS, 1984a). There was also much greater use of female birth control methods. The pill and the IUD were used by only 21 per cent of my sample but by 35 per cent of the FPIS sample. In contrast, the number of couples using the sheath had halved, and use of withdrawal and the safe perod was only a quarter of what it was at first intercourse. So, intercourse later in the relationship is likely to be with more effective, female-oriented birth control methods.

Communication on sexual matters   Although there may be less guilt about sexuality these days, it still exists and can result in a lack of communication about sexual matters. This may be a factor in the non-use of birth control and a resulting unwanted pregnancy. Respondents were asked 'How many of the following have you discussed birth control with, (if any)?' The data in Table 4.16 show that 95 per cent of the sample had discussed birth control with someone and three-quarters of the total had discussed it with their partner. However, there seems to be little family discussion, which may not be surprising given the general lack of discussion on even such basic functions as the menstrual period. Only just over a third of the British

Table 4.16 People with whom the sample had discussed birth control

Relationship	No.	%
no one	32	5.3
father	38	6.3
mother	220	36.2
brother	28	4.6
sister	153	25.2
girlfriend	267	43.9
teacher	24	3.9
partner	456	75.0
other	79	13.0

Note: Non-respondents excluded.

women discussed birth control with their mother and this figure was lower for the unmarried. In some cases, respondents even felt that their pregnancy might not have occurred if they could have had more family support. A 16 year old who was pregnant due to a condom failure said, for example: 'My pregnancy was caused through failure of contraceptive method, but also the lack of understanding from my parents who would of disagreed and not listened if I'd of asked them about the pill.'

A 20 year old who had been having intercourse for a year said she was using withdrawal because she was 'worried about side effects and the thought of anyone finding out I have sex, e.g. parents finding pill'. She further commented:

I was brought up in quite a religious family but we didn't attend church. However, although my parents talked freely about most things, they didn't discuss contraception and my mother was ill when it mattered most so I didn't have her to guide me. Sex happened, I felt guilty, I didn't want to acknowledge my loss of virginity by taking contraception. However, I've learned my lesson for myself.

The respondents were also asked 'How many of the following have you told about your pregnancy, (if any)?'. They were then provided with a list. A total of 609 of the sample replied to the question and this includes 150 of the married

Table 4.17 People with whom the sample had discussed their pregnancy

Relationship	Married		Not married		All	
	No.	%	No.	%	No.	%
father	13	8.6	95	20.7	108	17.7
mother	32	21.3	148	32.2	180	29.5
no one	2	1.3	21	4.6	23	3.8
brother	6	4.0	47	10.2	53	8.7
sister	26	17.3	97	21.1	123	20.2
girlfriend	36	24.0	202	44.0	238	39.1
partner	124	82.7	350	76.3	474	77.8
other	3	2.0	71	15.5	74	12.2

Note: Non-respondents to questions on marital status or relationship to confidant excluded. 'Not-married' includes the widowed, divorced and separated.

women living with their husbands. Table 4.17 shows that about 17 per cent of the married women had not told their husband about their pregnancy. This may well be because the husband might not approve of the abortion or because it could lead to complications in their personal life. A 30-year-old woman commented:

My husband is not the father. Husband had vasectomy as no alternative contraception available to us. Became pregnant on coil first time and cap the second time. This was a moment's indiscretion. I am unable to take the pill due to varicose veins and phlebitis.

Overall, just under 30 per cent of the women had told their mother about the pregnancy. The married women were less likely to inform them than the single women (only one in five doing so). The sample contained twenty-five older women who were widowed, divorced or separated and only two of these had informed their mother. If we exclude these to leave us with the single women under the age of 35, then just over a third had told their mother about their pregnancy.

Some people expected to tell their mother at a later date. So a 23-year-old single woman working as a dancer said: 'I shall inform my mother of the abortion in due course. I never agreed with abortion – it's a very sad and serious situation to be in, and I have every intention of making sure it never happens a second time'.

The total data on communication between parents and children show that both the older and younger generations still have difficulty in discussing their sexuality and possible problems they are facing. This lack of communication could indicate that there is a social problem that should be addressed. We have certainly seen that the sizeable minority of those parents who do not discuss sexual matters with their children cannot rely on the school to do it.

The use of birth control   One of the main aims in this survey was to show up gaps in knowledge and practice of birth control. Respondents were asked 'At the time you became pregnant, were you, or your partner, thinking of using a birth control method, using a method sometimes, always using a method, not using a method'. The replies are given in Table 4.18. After the non-response has been redistributed, the results show that in the sample as a whole two out of five women were always protected by birth control. A further quarter were protected sometimes. Of the 36 per cent who did not use birth control, nearly 10 per cent were thinking of doing so.

It seemed possible that those in more stable relationships would be more likely to have used birth control, so a special breakdown was prepared by marital status. The results are shown in Table 4.19. They show that just over half the married women were always using a method of birth control compared to just over a third of the total sample.

Table 4.18   Birth control use at conception

Use	No.	%	Corrected %
thinking of using	54	8.3	9.2
sometimes using	146	22.5	24.9
always using	230	35.4	39.3
not using	156	24.0	26.6
not known	63	9.8	
Total	649	100.0	100.0

Table 4.19   Birth control use at conception by marital status

Use	Married		Single		Widowed/ divorced/ separated	
	No.	%	No.	%	No.	%
thinking of using	9	6.5	41	10.7	4	6.1
sometimes using	33	23.9	97	25.4	16	24.2
always using	72	52.2	136	35.6	22	33.3
not using	24	17.4	108	28.3	24	36.4
Total	138	100.0	382	100.0	66	100.0

Note: Non-respondents excluded. 'Single' includes those of unknown marital status.

An interesting factor in birth control use is that of age and so a separate analysis was carried out on the young (which is discussed later) and on both the over 35s and the over 40s. Here some striking results were found. Of those over the age of 35, 38 per cent had always used birth control, which is slightly higher than for the sample as a whole. However, within the 35–39 age group, there was totally different usage by the married and the single women: 63 per cent of the forty-three married women used birth control compared to only 16 per cent of the twenty-five women who were widowed, divorced or separated. Amongst the fourteen women over the age of 40, neither the married nor the single were very assiduous in their use of birth control, and only two of them said they were always using it. One woman aged 48 said that at her age she thought it improbable she would become pregnant. Probably equally surprised was a 40-year-old woman who had become pregnant by her 67-year-old husband after three years of not taking precautions. She called her attitude 'a triumph of wishful thinking over reason and logic'.

There seem to be two sets of problems as far as older women are concerned. The older women with no regular relationship may not see the necessity for keeping their birth control practices together. They will probably be advised to go off the pill and may not get other protection. When they do meet partners it may well be that these have been used to women

Table 4.20 Reasons for not using birth control

Reason	No.	% of respondents
thought sterile	21	5.8
had intercourse unexpectedly	147	40.4
cost	3	0.8
did not know of any	3	0.8
did not know where to go	12	3.3
intended to use but had not made an appointment	62	17.0
religion says it is wrong	10	2.7
stopped using because of side effects	108	29.7
hoped pregnancy would lead to marriage	8	2.2
did not intend to have intercourse anymore	30	8.2

Note: calculations based on 364 respondents. Non-respondents and those pregnant through birth control failure excluded. Percentages add to more than 100 owing to multiple responses.

protecting themselves and may not therefore enquire too deeply into the woman's practice. There may also be some prejudice amongst older men against the condom, as they have usually spent a number of years without having to take such precautions. There may therefore be a need to direct some educational and advertising programmes towards this group. The second problem is the lack of knowledge about end of the fertile period.

Background to non-use of birth control We asked the women in the sample who had not used birth control for the reason. Their replies are given in Table 4.20, which shows that by far the commonest reason given for non-use of birth control was that they had 'had intercourse unexpectedly'. This is a particular problem when women first begin to have sex or when they have been out of a regular relationship for some time. Young women might imagine that sexuality is wrong for them, but sometimes they do not meet their own standards of behaviour. Anyone in this position will not wish to go and get protection because that would imply acceptance of a part of their sexuality that they do not wish to recognise. Three out of ten of the sample said they had 'stopped using because of side-effects', which suggests that many of those giving up the pill are slow in making use of the alternative sources of birth control. Some of the replies show the individual problems that have led women to choose abortions. For example, eight said they had hoped pregnancy would lead to marriage. A 27-year-old unemployed woman commented:

> I have always used birth control of some sort or other. I have been on the pill for over 10 years up until just before last Christmas when my boyfriend started suggesting marriage and we decided we would like children. However, when I found out that I was pregnant my boyfriend and I had been going through a rough patch, and he found another woman who he has since married. This is why I have to have an abortion. He feels if I kept the child it would ruin his life and his marriage.

Birth control failure   Those suspecting failure of their birth control method were asked the method they used. Table 4.21 gives some indication of the effectiveness of different methods of birth control in practice. It shows, for example, that only 7 per cent of couples in the FPIS United Kingdom sample use withdrawal or the safe period as their method of birth control and yet these methods accounted for three cases out of ten of patients for abortion in my sample. So these 'natural' methods are four times over-represented compared to their overall usage – although we should note that these methods were probably used to a greater degree by the younger groups, who are most at risk for an abortion. This factor also applies to the sheath, which accounted for nearly 37 per cent of birth control failures but is used by only 19 per cent of the population. The diaphragm (cap) is also over-represented in the percentage of failures, and this may often be due to user failure. The only methods under-represented in terms of failure are sterilisation, the pill and the IUD.

Various women in the sample complained about the quality of birth control devices available. A 42-year-old married woman who became pregnant after using the safe period commented:

Table 4.21 Pregnancy because of birth control failure

Method of birth control	Survey sample No. of failures	%	UK usage of method %
pill	53	17.6	35
IUD	18	5.9	10
cap (diaphragm)	27	8.9	1
sheath	111	36.6	19
withdrawal	54	17.8	} 7
safe period	36	11.9	
foam	4	1.3	—
sterilisation	—	—	28
Total	303	100	100

Sources: FPIS (1984a) and this survey.
Note: Non-respondents excluded.

I feel rather frustrated not finding a suitable contraceptive method. The pill is not suitable for me because of my smoking, age and varicose veins. The coil I don't trust, the cap I have tried, but not suitable for me. My decision to have an abortion I feel was the right one for me definitely and I am glad to have had a choice. However, I did have very strong feelings of anger and depression having to make the decision in the first place.

A 21-year-old single woman became pregnant after using the safe period and a condom at times when not safe. She commented:

I was advised to stop using the pill after $3\frac{1}{2}$ years because of severe side effects (vaginal infections, thrush, cystitis – very bad). Due to my severe attack of cystitis my doctor advised me not to use any contraception except Durex. Neither I nor my boyfriend liked this so I tried to find out about the safe period. So I read some books on the different methods, and used the calendar and mucus method (no one gave me a thermometer). This worked well for a year (I didn't get pregnant or cystitis). Then I went on holiday to Africa. I don't know whether I miscalculated the safe period, whether the change in climate upset my body. I did not want to be pregnant, and, although I was very upset when I found out, I never considered not terminating it (not seriously anyway).

A 34-year-old married woman, pregnant after a failure of withdrawal, stated:

> I am disappointed that there is not enough choice in contraception. I did not like the coil because it was very painful at period time so I had it taken out. The pill I do not agree with so I am going to try the cap.

A number of women suffered birth control failure while on the pill. One's failure occurred when she changed her brand. Another, a 24-year-old married woman, had conflicting medication. She commented: 'I think that the fact I was on a course of antibiotics and was not told to take some other form of precaution was terrible thus leading to my pregnancy and termination.' A 20-year-old single woman living with her parents had similar problems after regular pill usage:

> I was on the pill regularly but no one told me that simple things like sickness can stop pill action. I feel that, if there are more cases like this, then doctors should be advised to give more information on the pill to their patients.

However, the usual reason for pill failure was that there had been some lack of use. Typical comments were: 'Using the pill. Forgot one night, took it too late the next day'; 'I became pregnant because I missed three of my pills'; 'I was taking the pill regularly but through accident forgot to take it. This is why I became pregnant.'

The highest number of failures of birth control was due to the condom. A 30-year-old married woman commented: 'My pregnancy was an accident. The condom was used but it slipped off.' A number of women complained that their condoms had burst or split. One woman unable to use the pill or IUD said she had had six condoms burst in the previous two years. Two of the respondents, pregnant after a condom had split, commented that they wished they had known about after-sex birth control. This has, of course, been a controversial area because some birth control providers have been concerned that some people would use after-sex birth control regularly instead of taking the usual precautions. Their suspicions are not without some foundation. One of the respondents in the sample said that she wished she had known that the morning-after pill shouldn't be used more than once in the month. However, there seems to be a good case for providing regular attenders at family planning clinics with a morning-after pill so that if they check a condom and it has broken they can take immediate remedial action.

There were a few failures on the cap. One woman said that she was definitely on the cap at the time of pregnancy and that she had not had a weight change in the previous year so the size of her appliance was presumably correct, but still she became pregnant. Others, however, felt they were partially at fault in their pregnancy. One said that she had failed to check the cap was in place after going horse riding and a 32-year-old divorced woman said that she had not had the size checked for two years when she should have had it checked every six months.

There were a disproportionate number of failures of the safe period. Its largely Catholic advocates have been arguing that when combined with evidence from mucus analysis as proposed by Billings it is effective. However, the evidence suggests that for many people the degree of restraint involved is likely to lead to unwanted pregnancies. My survey showed that many who use the safe period do so in combination with the condom at the most dangerous times.

Repeat abortions The respondents were asked 'Have you had any previous abortions? If so, please specify how many.' Table 4.22 shows that on the raw data just over three-quarters had no previous abortions. However, the non-response on this question was a little higher than on the questions immediately following it (the three subsequent questions having an average non-response of fourteen). So it seems safe to assume that some of the women in the survey who had not had any abortions did not see the need to answer the question. The correction for non-response therefore shows that more than four-fifths of the sample were in for their first abortion. As the problem of repeat abortions is one that recurs we carried out further analysis of the subject.

Table 4.22 Previous abortions for the total sample

Previous abortions	No.	%	Corrected %
none	492	75.8	81.9
one	98	15.1	15.4
two	14	2.2	2.2
three	1	0.2	0.2
four	2	0.3	0.3
not known/none	42	6.5	
Total	649	100.0	100.0

Table 4.23 Repeat abortions and marital status

Status	First abortion		Second abortion		Third or more abortion	
	No.	%	No.	%	No.	%
married	127	26.2	28	29.2	4	30.8
single	311	64.3	53	55.2	4	30.8
widowed	2	0.4	2	2.1	—	—
separated	18	3.7	5	5.2	2	15.4
divorced	26	5.4	8	8.3	3	23.1
Total	485	100	96	100	13	100

Note: Non-respondents to questions on marital status or repeat abortion excluded.

Comparing Table 4.23 with Table 4.7 reveals that there was a little variation according to marital status. The single women were slightly over-represented amongst those having their first abortion, and considerably under-represented in the multiple-abortion category, while the married women were slightly over-represented in the multiple abortion category. However, it was the widowed, divorced and separated who had the greatest over-representation among those having had previous abortions (30.3 per cent had had a previous one). This may be related to certain problems of birth control use within this group, as has been discussed.

Those women who have had more than one abortion may well be those who have found particular problems with birth control methods. They may also mention the difficulty of obtaining a sterilisation. A 24-year-old married woman commented:

> I have had many problems with contraceptives (side effects from pill, I.U.D. falling out, sheath failing, etc.) resulting in my becoming pregnant 3 times against my wishes. Also I have a son which my husband and I planned, but desire no more children. Because of this my husband and I have decided that it would be best if I were sterilised. However, despite our continual requests since the birth of my son, every source has turned us down (NHS, BPAS) and now I have become pregnant again and yet still I have been turned down. Why??? We are trying to be sensible and no one will help.

Sterilisation involves difficult decisions and the medical practitioners sometimes feel a responsibility towards a longer view. Some of the problems are discussed by Allen (1985).

One of the questions to ask about repeat abortion is whether the group contained a disproportionate percentage of careless women or whether those presenting for a second or subsequent abortion had largely been unlucky in terms of contraceptive failure. Birth control use was therefore compared to the number of abortions. Table 4.24 shows that two in five of the women in for their first abortion had always used birth control and that the percentage rose slightly for those in for their second abortion. In fact, only just over one in five of the women having their second abortion were not using birth control at all. This suggests that the group contained a disproportionate percentage of women who had had 'bad luck' in terms of birth control failure. However, when the group of women presenting for their third or more abortion is considered, it can be seen that only one in five were always using birth control. This was a small group and so it is important not to draw too many conclusions. However, the survey suggests there may be a group of women and their partners who continue to ignore the necessity of regular birth control to prevent unwanted pregnancies.

I carried out a further analysis to see if the women seeking repeat abortions had begun their sex at an earlier age than the

Table 4.24 Repeat abortions and birth control use at conception

Birth control use	First abortion		Second abortion		Third or more abortion	
	No.	%	No.	%	No.	%
thinking of using birth control	43	9.6	6	6.5	2	14.3
using a method sometimes	99	22.2	31	33.7	7	50.0
always using a method	177	39.7	40	43.5	3	21.4
not using a method	127	28.5	15	16.3	2	14.3
Total	446	100	92	100	14	100

Note: Non-respondents to questions on birth control use or repeat abortion excluded.

others. The results showed that those in for their second abortion began their sexual activity later than those in for their first. However, the fourteen women in for their third abortion or more had tended to begin their intercourse at an earlier age than both the other groups.

Catholics for abortion Because the Catholic Church has been so assiduous in opposing both birth control and abortion, I carried out a special analysis of the Catholic sub-group. One of the points of interest was whether those having abortions were those who had lapsed from their religion. A previous survey I carried out amongst 1,000 New York students had shown that the regular church attenders were much more likely to be anti-abortion than those who had attended less frequently (Francome 1984a). In this survey, respondents were asked 'Have you been to a place of worship recently?' They were then given a list such as 'past week' to complete their response. The results are shown in Table 4.25. Catholics were more than three times as likely to have been to church in the previous week in comparison with the rest of the sample. If the 'not knowns' are redistributed, then two-fifths of the Catholics had been to church in the previous month. So it does seem that a sizeable minority of the Catholic women were reasonably regular

Table 4.25   Catholic church attendance compared to rest of sample

Last attendance	Catholics No.	%	Non-Catholics No.	%
past week	13	16.0	26	4.6
past month	17	21.0	80	14.1
past year	23	28.4	118	20.8
not in past year	22	27.2	290	51.0
not known	6	7.4	54	9.5
Total	81	100.0	568	100.0

Note: 'Non Catholic' includes those of unknown religion

church attenders. Indeed, only one in four had not been to a religious service in the previous year, which suggests that those who had totally broken from the Church were a relatively small minority.

Sometimes the questionnaires revealed evidence of conflict over abortion. Thus a 17-year-old single Catholic who had been to church in the past week commented:

> Even though I have been through an abortion I would like others not to use abortion as another form of contraceptive. For abortion is not preventing a birth but killing an individual, even though some people disagree. At conception life begins; abortion takes place after conception and people should remember that. Abortion is a serious matter and should be treated so, especially by those terminating a baby. Even though I have had an abortion, I hope and pray I never have to go through it again for moral and emotional reasons.

On the other hand, another respondent who was 21 years old and had also been to church in the previous week adopted a more aggressive approach:

> I come from Ireland and I know for a fact that if people faced reality there, they would see so many young people ruining their lives by being pushed into marriage because they are pregnant and ruining their lives, their husband's and their babies. They think that by having no clinics like these that

young girls will be afraid to get pregnant and won't have intercourse, which is rubbish! There is so many children battered and beaten because their parents cannot stand the pressures and are too young to be able to cope with life!

A third woman, 28 years old, pregnant because of a coil failure, and at church in the previous two weeks, commented at the individual level:

I am grateful that there is a choice you can make in whether having a child or not and for me a termination was inevitable because of circumstances as I am already a one parent family.

Some surveys have shown Catholics having a disproportionately high percentage of abortions. I certainly found this in my earlier studies in New York and Boston. Some commentators have drawn attention to the fact that the Church opposes artificial birth control and that this may inhibit the sexually active from taking precautions (Francome, 1984a). In this sample, however, Catholics were roughly in proportion to the national proportion of Catholics overall.

The comments written on the questionnaires did, however, show some evidence of conflicts over birth control use. Thus a single Catholic from Aberdeen, who had been to church in the past week and was pregnant after she and her boyfriend had been using withdrawal, commented: 'I never used birth control because of my religion. But when I fell pregnant the first thing that came into my mind was to have an abortion. So now I have made up my mind to use birth control, so I don't have to go through this again.' Others had written comments such as 'Never have used any birth control' and 'I do not agree with female methods of birth control', although only one in twenty reported they had not used birth control because their religion said it was wrong.

A few commentators have dubbed the rhythm method 'Vatican roulette'. Many couples, and especially Catholics, practise a variation of this 'condom roulette' whereby they use nothing during the safe period but instead of abstaining during the fertile period use a condom. A single 21 year old commented: 'On the rare occasions when my boyfriend and I have intercourse we usually use a sheath unless I think it especially safe not to. When I became pregnant this time it was because the sheath broke. I can say this confidently because intercourse is *very* rare betweeen us.' The advantage of this 'condom roulette' is that those practising it are breaking the rules of the Church on birth control less frequently. However, it can be problematical in that confusion over dates can easily lead to an unwanted pregnancy. Overall most British Catholics have not followed the teachings of the Church on birth control. Those who have may in certain circumstances suffer an unwanted pregnancy and choose an abortion, as has been seen. However, these are possibly balanced by the few Catholics totally opposed to abortion.

Teenage pregnancy and abortion   There has been a great deal of debate in Britain on the question of teenage sexuality and pregnancy. One view is that sex education for teenagers has been counterproductive in that it encourages them to think about sex and leads to an increase in promiscuity. Furthermore, because there is no comparable increase in birth control, the solution can in fact make the problem worse. This view has been propounded with a great deal of success by organisations like the Responsible Society and anti-abortion organisations like the Society for the Protection of Unborn Children. For example, Joana Bogle wrote an article in the *Daily Mail* (7 September 1981) in which she argued that many of the 'sex experts' who campaigned so enthusiastically in the late 1960s and early 1970s for more sex education in schools and advice on birth control as the answer to teenage pregnancy were admitting that they might have made a great mistake. In 1979, she stated, the number of live births to unmarried women was almost 24,000 higher than at the start of the decade. She went on to argue that the number of abortions had also increased. Bogle's figures are misleading because they do not take into account the increase in the number of teenagers during the period considered, and it is clearly the *rate* of births and pregnancy that is most relevant. Moreover, they do not account for the great fall in so-called 'shotgun' marriages that occurred in the 1970s and early 1980s.

Some politicians have been influenced by those who say sex education has failed. For example, most of the media carried comments on sexuality made by Mrs Thatcher (26 July 1982): 'In family matters today there are some disquieting features. For example in 1882 there were 43,000 illegitimate births in England and Wales. Some 80 years later, in 1960, there were approximately the same number. In 1980 the number had risen to 77,000.' Here again the impression is given of great social dislocation caused by promiscuous behaviour. In fact, as I pointed out to Mrs Thatcher in a letter, the illegitimacy rate fell between 1960 and 1980 (Francome, 1984b). Mrs Thatcher is not alone in accepting the view that indicators of sexual dislocation are getting worse. When Gerard Vaughan was Minister of Health, Joanna Nash suggested to him that contraceptive-oriented policies were not successful. She reported that his face registered despair and then he said: 'It hasn't worked has it? I just don't know the answer.' Later in the interview he said that sex education should be left in the hands of parents and that people leave too much to the state (*Universe*, 29 August 1980).

In fact, the evidence of recent years shows that the advocates of sex education are having increasing success. The age-specific birthrates for teenagers in postwar years show a number of trends but two main ones are evident. Between 1951 and 1961 there was a rise in births from 21 per 1,000 women under the age of 20 to 37 per 1,000 (Francome, 1984b). This rise continued to 48 per 1,000 in 1966 and 51 per 1,000 in 1971. However, the trend then reversed and there was a marked fall in the birthrate to 28 per 1,000 in 1982. In a previous article I carried out a detailed analysis of the changes during the decade 1970–9 (Francome, 1983). This covered much of the period when the 1967 Abortion Act was first in operation. Over the seven years 1971–7 inclusive, the birthrate for women under the age of 20 fell from 51.5 to 30.0 per 1,000. So the fall in births was 21.5 per 1,000. The abortion rate increased over the period, but only from 12.1 per 1,000 to 15.1 per 1,000. So only one-seventh of the fall in births can be attributed to an increase in the number of abortions. With the scare about the pill in 1977 there was a slight rise in births but the trend has since begun to move downwards again.

It seems that this reduction in births has occurred despite an increase in teenage sexuality. Two surveys that spanned part of the period were those of Schofield (1965) and Farrell (1978). Their figures were not immediately comparable because Schofield excluded married teenagers and Farrell included them. However, in an earlier article I reworked the data to show that the percentage of teenagers saying they had had intercourse increased greatly during the period (Francome, 1979). Schofield carried out his survey in 1964 and Farrell completed her study in 1975. In 1964, 5 per cent of unmarried 16-year-old women said they had had intercourse; by 1974/5 this had quadrupled to 21 per cent. The percentage of 18-year-old females saying they had had intercourse almost tripled from 17 per cent in 1964 to 47 per cent in 1974/5. In all age groups the teenage males said they had experienced sexual intercourse more frequently than the females. However, over the period the percentage of girls saying they had had intercourse increased faster than that for the boys, so the gap closed somewhat. Although some of the reported change in behaviour is likely to be due to teenagers being more willing to report their experiences, and although these studies cover only part of the period, it is reasonable to assume some increase in teenage sexuality during the period 1970–7 and that the marked decline in teenage births was largely due to a much greater use of birth control.

Sex, birth control and the younger teenagers In some societies teenage births are accepted as the norm but in Britain this is much less so. A study in Bristol showed that two-thirds of pregnancies going to term were unplanned. This would suggest a national proportion of nearly 40,000 in 1981 and a total of around 80,000 unplanned teenage pregnancies (FPIS, 1984b, p.3). A crucial factor influencing the outcome of a teenage pregnancy is the woman's age, as is clear from Table 4.26. The figures show that for teenagers aged 15 and under nearly three-quarters of the pregnancies end in abortion. As age increases there is a steady decline in the percentage, until by the age of nineteen it is only one in four. A proportion of the older teenagers will be in stable relationships and may well have decided that they want to start a family. The latest data for those aged 15 years in England and Wales are for 1982 and they show an abortion rate of 7.43 per 1,000 and a birth rate of 2.42 (*Hansard*, 8 November 1983).

Table 4.26   Outcome of pregnancy for teenagers, 1980

Age	Abortions per 100 pregnancies
15 and under	73.9
16	59.5
17	42.5
18	31.4
19	25.0
Total under 20	36.7

Source: Francome (1984b)

The legal position of teenagers aged 16–18 differs from the situation in the United States. The British 1969 Family Law Reform Act, which reduced the age of majority from 21 to 18, also allowed young people aged 16 to consent to their own surgical, medical or dental treatment without obtaining the consent of parents, provided that the issues involved are understood. Women at family planning clinics are asked if they have any objection to their doctor being informed. As far as the under-sixteens are concerned, the decision whether or not to prescribe contraception for a person under the age of 16 without parental consent rests ultimately with the doctor. The original advice on the doctors' legal position was provided in a Department of Health and Social Security (DHSS) Family Planning Service Memorandum of Guidance in May 1974. This stated that the doctor was 'not acting unlawfully provided he [sic] acts in good faith in protecting the girl against the harmful effects of intercourse.' This ruling was challenged by a Catholic mother of ten, Mrs Victoria Gillick, who wanted parental rights restored. She lost the first court case in 1983, won the appeal in 1984 but finally lost in the House of Lords in October 1985, when the Department of Health and Social Security challenged the Appeal Court ruling. A few days before the ruling Mrs Gillick attacked the Catholic hierarchy for their lack of support. By three votes to two the Law Lords decided a doctor would be justified in counselling or treating an under 16 year old without parental consent in certain circumstances. These were:

- that she would understand the doctor's advice;
- that she could not be persuaded to inform her parents or permit them to be informed;
- that she is very likely to begin to or continue to have sexual intercourse with or without contraceptive advice;
- that unless she receives contraceptive advice or treatment her physical or mental health are likely to suffer;
- that it is in her best interest to receive birth control either with or without parental consent (Simpson, 1985)

In this survey, I carried out a special analysis of the thirty-six women aged 16 and under presenting for abortion. Ten of the thirty-six were actually under the age of 16 and all except one were white. Other observers have suggested that participants in sex during the early teens are disproportionately from the working class. The background of my sample, based on the Registrar General's classification of occupations, is shown in Table 4.27. Only eight of the fathers and five of the mothers had middle-class occupations, which is somewhat below what we would expect. One in seven had no father present, because he was either deceased or missing for other reasons.

Those who argue that birth control advice encourages teenage sex must find little support from our figures. Overall there is the impression of lack of birth control usage. Only one-third of this sub-sample used any kind of birth control at first intercourse, with six using mechanical methods – five used a sheath and one the pill – and a further five using withdrawal and one using the safe period. At the time of conception, only

Table 4.27   Social class and the under sixteens

Social class	Father	Mother
upper middle	1	0
lower middle	7	5
upper working	11	4
lower working	7	12
no job	3	13
deceased/no father	2	2
not known	2	2
Total	36	36

one in six of those responding always used birth control and one in four used birth control sometimes. Half were not using birth control at all. When those not using birth control were asked the reason for non-use, two-thirds (eighteen) said they had intercourse unexpectedly. In the next highest category were the seven who said they had intended to use birth control but had not made the appointment; a further two said they did not intend to have intercourse any more and two thought they were sterile. Presumably in the latter case they felt they were too young to become pregnant. This suggests that amongst very young teenagers sex is unplanned and largely unanticipated. A pertinent factor is the age at first intercourse and the age of partner. These data are given in Table 4.28, which shows that the eight teenagers who had first intercourse at the age of 14 had partners whose average age was also below the legal minimum. The age gap rises as the age of first intercourse rises. This indicates a problem of a few under-age girls and boys who become sexually active but, from the evidence of birth control usage, with little responsibility or concern for the possible consequences.

However, it does seem that once a crisis has arisen the youngest teenagers are the ones most likely to fall back on their family relationships. The youngest group was the one in our sample most likely to inform their family about the pregnancy: three-quarters (twenty-seven) had told their mothers and half (seventeen) had told their father.

Although the numbers involved are relatively small, the evidence does suggest a need for special consideration of younger teenagers, who have so far not responded to sex education with a reduced rate of unwanted pregnancy.

Table 4.28   Age at first intercourse for young abortion patients

Age	No.	Av. age of partner
14 years	8	15.4
15 years	12	17.9
16 years	16	19.6

Abortion amongst immigrant groups   The two major immigrant groups in Britain face many challenges and problems and nowhere is this clearer than in the area of sexuality, marriage and the family. Those from the Indian subcontinent came with marriage and family patterns very different from not only the indigenous population but also those of West Indian origin. For example, Asian women are much more likely to stop at home rather than to work: in 1977 for women over the age of 16 only 12 per cent of those originating from Bangladesh and 19 per cent of those from Pakistan were in paid employment – in contrast to a figure of 47 per cent for the total UK population and 74 per cent for women of West Indian origin (OPCS, 1980). There are also educational differences between the ethnic groups, which are likely to be increasingly reflected in status terms in the long term. The differences are particularly great amongst the men: recent reports suggest that almost one-quarter of Asian men finish their education after the age of 20 compared with 7 per cent of white and 2 per cent of West Indian men. More Asian men are self-employed than members of the other groups (*New Society*, 1 November 1984).

For Asian teenagers of both sexes the tradition of arranged marriages is a source of potential conflict. They have seen their school friends or others in the indigenous population exercising free will in terms of their marital selection, while they have often been pressed into a relationship with someone they did not know. Those of us counselling and teaching Asian-born students encounter the situation daily. I am good friends with a nearby Pakistani family in which two of the sons are students. I went on holiday for a week and when I returned I found I had missed two weddings. The eldest son was told on the Wednesday that he was to be married on the Saturday and the dowry money was used to marry one of his sisters the following day. They have both accepted the situation. However, a younger brother who moved around a great deal while training to be a doctor has continual arguments with his father as he wants to choose his own bride. His girlfriend is living in Pakistan and he plans to marry her, but his father feels this is a slight. A much more traumatic situation has occurred with another student who was living in a stable relationship with his Asian girlfriend. His parents brought someone else for him to marry from India and he refused and there was a great deal of conflict. One day he told me he was not getting on well with his family and 'I forgot to go to my wedding on Saturday'. It turned out that, as the young girl was about to be sent home unmarried, he had agreed to a marriage of convenience while another partner was found for her. However, he had then decided against attending the wedding and his family was very upset, especially his father's brother in India who had made the arrangements for the trip. At the time of writing he is under great conflict whether to stand by his girlfriend, who he would have married with parental approval, or whether to give in to family pressure and move home. His sister has five daughters and she feels that if her brother does not accept the traditional patterns of marriage it will make it difficult for her to arrange a marriage for her children. So the families must decide how far they wish to adjust to the existing norms of English culture.

There are also clear problems within the Asian community in Britain in terms of sexuality. Virginity is highly prized and so those who have sex must keep it secret if they may want to enter the arranged marriage market at a later stage. A 20-year-old female Asian student told me that one of her friends had confided in her about the fact that she had an abortion. However, later when she was about to be married the woman said 'You had better forget about what I told you about the abortion because I made it up and it isn't true.'

The West Indian (black) immigrants have come from a colonial tradition at the polar extreme in terms of marriage patterns and sexual norms. With over 70 per cent of births occurring outside marriage in several West Indian islands, illegitimacy has a totally different connotation (Goode, 1964). The difference was shown clearly when *Social Trends* (1979, p.67) published figures for the birth practices of the major British groups. The overall illegitimacy rate for 1976 was 9 per cent but this figure masked the fact that the illegitimacy rate for women from the Indian subcontinent was 1 per cent, while that for the black West Indian immigrants was 48 per cent. The figures also showed that within the Asian community over a quarter (27 per cent) of the births were of the fourth or higher order within marriage, compared to a national figure of 7 per cent.

Table 4.29 Relationship with partner by ethnic group

Relationship	Asian No.	%	Black No.	%	White No.	%
casual	1	4	6	24	81	14
steady	7	25	14	56	370	62
fiancé	—	—	—	—	122	20
other	—	—	—	—	10	2
husband to be	16	57	1	4	3	0
not known	4	14	4	17	10	2
Total	28	100	25	100	596	100

Note: The few women of Chinese or other origin are included under 'white' in this table and the rest of this section. 'White' also includes those of unknown ethnic group.

This kind of evidence led me to expect wide differences in my sample among the Asian and black groups and the indigenous population, and indeed that is just what the results did show. Possibly the clearest difference was in terms of the relationship of the partner at first intercourse, which is shown in Table 4.29. The sample contained nineteen Asian women who were currently married or had been married: fifteen of these said they had their first intercourse with their 'husband to be' or their husband, three did not respond to the question, and one said first intercourse resulted from a steady relationship. This contrasts to the situation for other groups where, out of 146 married women, only four had their first intercourse with their husband or 'husband to be'.

Twenty-three of the Asian women responded to the question about first information about the menstrual period. Just under half (eleven) received the first information from their mother, while nearly a third (seven) had not known what to expect. The results from the black women was similar in terms of receiving information from their mother: nine of the nineteen respondents to the question were told first by their mother. However, only one in five had no information at all. There was some suggestion from the survey results that black women matured at an earlier average age than Asian women: just over half of the Asian women had their first period before the age of

Table 4.30   Age at first intercourse by ethnic group

Age	Asian No.	%	Black No.	%	White No.	%
15 or under	2	7.5	2	9	72	12
16–17	6	23	5	22	258	45
18–19	6	23	11	48	169	29
20–24	8	31	4	17	73	13
25–29	2	7.5	1	4	4	
30–34	1	4	—	—	2	1
35–39	1	4	—	—	1	
Total	26	100	23	100	577	100

Note: Nineteen white, two black and two Asian women did not respond to the question and were not included. 'White' includes those of unknown ethnic group.

14 compared to nearly three-quarters of the blacks. The numbers in the sample are too small for me to be definitive on the matter, but it may be a fruitful area of research for others to consider.

It might be expected from the information about partners that there would be a difference between the ethnic groups in age at first intercourse. Table 4.30 shows that whites in the sample began their sexual intercourse at an earlier age than both the other groups: over half the whites had their first intercourse by the age of 17 compared to under a third of the two other groups. This result is statistically significant. Almost half (twelve) of the twenty-six Asians did not have their first intercourse until over the age of 20. This was a considerably higher proportion than both the other groups.

In the sample as a whole, I found that one in five of the married women and one in three of the single women said they discussed their pregnancy with their mother. Amongst the Asians only three, or one in nine, had told their mother, as had only one in five of the black women. So, although the figures are too small to make a definitive judgement, it seems that the general lack of discussion across the generations is accentuated amongst the non-white groups.

One might expect that the non-white groups, containing such a high percentage of immigrants, would be less able to avail themselves of the free birth control facilities. Their abortions might therefore be expected to be more due to lack of use rather than failure of method. There is some support for this from the data. Less than one in three (seven) of the Asian women had always used birth control compared to two-fifths of the total sample and over half the married women in the sample. The results for the blacks were similar. So, taking the two non-white groups together, fourteen had always used birth control out of a possible forty-five. Given the large number of higher order births amongst the immigrant groups it could well be the case that other unwanted pregnancies went to term and that a different approach to birth control might be advisable. In particular, those from ethnic groups where the women are seldom allowed out could benefit from an extension of services via district nurses visiting women in their homes.

Another of the problems for immigrant groups is that it may be very difficult for them to work their way through the British system to get an abortion. Statistics published in the confidential enquiries into maternal deaths strongly suggest that recent immigrants were having problems in obtaining safe legal abortions and were being forced into unsafe illegal ones. In the period 1970–5, more than half the women dying from illegal abortions were immigrants from the New Commonwealth. Their death rate from abortion was over ten times that of women born in this country (Francome, 1980).

Some people have argued that the two major non-white groupings in Britain should combine together and work for their rights. This research shows that any such attempt would need to recognise the wide differences between the groups and the separate kinds of problems they face.

Abortion in Scotland

The official data

Table 4.31 gives the figures for Scottish women having abortions in their own country. The data show only a slight increase in the number of abortions between 1971 and 1978.

Table 4.31   Scottish abortions, 1971–1983 ('000s)

	1971	1978	1979	1980	1981	1982	1983
married	3.3	2.9	3.0	2.8	3.0	2.6	—
single	2.4	3.7	3.8	4.2	4.9	4.8	—
widowed/divorced/ separated	0.6	0.8	1.0	0.9	1.1	1.0	—
all	6.3	7.4	7.8	7.9	9.0	8.4	8.4
Scottish women having abortions in England	1.0	0.9	1.0	1.2	1.0	0.9	0.8
rate per 1,000, 15–44	6.3	7.0	7.3	7.3	8.3	7.6	—
rate including those going to England	7.3	7.9	8.4	8.4	9.2	8.4	8.3

Source: Scottish Abstract of Statistics (HMSO), no. 13, 1984, p.21. Registrar General Scotland (1984).

Table 4.32   Abortion rates per 1,000 women aged 15–44 by marital status: Scotland, 1970–1982

Marital status	1970	1975	1980	1981	1982
married	4.1	4.6	4.3	4.6	4.0
single	5.9	9.8	10.7	12.4	12.4
Total	5.2	7.1	7.3	8.3	7.6

Sources: Registrar General Scotland (1984), p.127. The census does not distinguish 'separated' women so one cannot calculate the abortion rate for the widowed/divorced/separated group.

The rise from 7,400 in 1978 to 9,000 in 1981 suggests that there may well have been an effect from the move to less efficient forms of contraception. There was a substantial drop in abortions in 1982 and this level was maintained in 1983. Scotland has relatively few private abortions and so women not able to get an NHS operation may well decide to travel to England. In 1981, 998 Scottish residents had their abortion in England, in 1982, 898 did so and by 1983 the number had dropped to 814. By adding the figures for women travelling to England to the data for the home abortions, I calculated that Scotland had an overall abortion rate of 8.3 per 1,000 in 1983 in comparison with a rate of 11.9 for England and Wales. Among countries with liberal laws, Scotland has the lowest abortion rate in the world except for Holland.

The major reason for the drop in the number of abortions in 1982 seems to be changing patterns amongst married women, as Table 4.32 shows. The abortion rate for married women dropped from 4.6 per 1,000 in 1981 to 4.0 in 1982. At this level the number of abortions is even lower than it was in 1970, just two years after the Abortion Act came into operation.

The abortion rate per 1,000 women varies greatly between regions. In 1982, Tayside, Lothian and Grampian had rates of 11.6, 9.8 and 9.2 per 1,000 women aged 15–44, respectively. In contrast, the rates for Argyll and Clyde, the Western Isles (1981) and Lanarkshire were 4.6, 4.9 and 5.0, respectively (Register General Scotland, 1984). One striking fact about Scottish abortions is that they entailed a mean stay in hospital of 3.7 days in 1980 and 2.3 days in 1981, which is in striking contrast to countries such as the United States and Holland where day care is the norm.

Scottish evidence from the sample survey

The data were collected from respondents in a hospital in Aberdeen. This is the town that pioneered many practices in Britain in the area of birth control and abortion, in many cases under the influence of Sir Dugald Baird. In 1946, Aberdeen Local Health Authority took over a birth control clinic started by Marie Stopes in the 1930s and birth control advice became available to all women as part of postnatal care (Baird, 1973). The abortion practice in Aberdeen was more liberal than most other places and under Scottish common law the decision was made to abort a woman if it were in her best interests. Baird reported 200 terminations between 1937 and 1947 and that during the period 1961–3 1.8 per cent of pregnancies to married women were terminated (Baird 1973, p.103). The pill was introduced in 1964, and between 1965 and 1969 there was a decrease of 25 per cent and 40 per cent respectively in the number of third and fourth order births. Birth control advice became free to all women referred by a doctor in 1970 – five years earlier than for the rest of the country.

Table 4.33   Birth control use at conception in Scotland and in England and Wales

| | Scotland | | | | England & Wales | | | |
| | Married | | Single | | Married | | Single | |
Use	No.	%	No.	%	No.	%	No.	%
thinking of using	0	0	5	12	9	7	40	10
sometimes using	0	0	8	19	33	26	105	26
always using	9	100	16	37	63	49	142	35
not using	0	0	14	32	24	18	118	29
Total	9	100	43	100	129	100	405	100

Note: Non-respondents excluded. 'Single' includes those of unknown marital status.

With this background of birth control availability and Scotland's overall lower abortion rate it was clearly of interest to see if the results from my fifty-three Scottish respondents showed any marked differences from the rest of the sample. As in the rest of Britain, in three cases out of five the Scottish women first learned about the menstrual cycle from their mother. However, only 18 per cent of the Scots had no knowledge of what to expect, compared to a quarter of the total sample. The age of first intercourse for Scotland was comparable with that for the rest of the population: half of them had had their first intercourse by the age of 17, compared to 55 per cent of the total sample. The relationship with their first partner was also similar to that of the rest of Britain. So it seems that the main influence on the lower abortion rate is to be found in birth control usage at time of conception. The data in Table 4.33 show that although the sample of married women in Scotland was small (there were only nine of them), they without exception became pregnant because of a failure of method: there were six condom failures, two pill and one withdrawal. This compares with a figure of just under half for the rest of Britain. Birth control usage amongst the non-married seems to have been much less regular, with only sixteen out of forty-three always using birth control. Despite the relatively small numbers involved, there is a clear statistical difference between the single and married. Of the twenty-seven single women who had not always used birth control, just over half said they had had intercourse unexpectedly. So it can be seen that there are problems in Scotland as in the rest of Britain with intercourse for which people are unprepared. Overall though, the Scottish tradition of birth control usage seems an important factor in keeping the abortion rate lower than it is in the rest of Britain.

Conclusion

The data in this chapter show that over the past decade there has been a great deal of improvement in the effectiveness of birth control, especially amongst teenagers. However, I have identified many areas where there could be further progress.

First of all there are clearly great gaps in terms of sex education. For one-quarter of women in the sample to say that they did not know what to expect when their periods arrived is very disquieting. Many people have expressed the view that basic sex education should be left to parents, but my evidence shows that they are not fulfilling this role. Furthermore, in many families there are great problems in terms of the discussion of sexuality, so the schools are the obvious alternative. Those opposed to sex education in schools and the availability of birth control have advanced the argument that it will encourage sexual activity and may well make matters worse. My evidence about the lack of birth control at the earliest ages and its success in reducing unwanted pregnancies amongst teenagers indicates that sex education can play an important role. It is a strange society that teaches its young about the latest developments in science, introduces them to computers and provides facts about the various countries of the world but does not give them the basic information about the workings of their own bodies and treats sex as if it were covered by the Official Secrets Act. It may well be that some local school teachers are uncomfortable about sex education, and given the general concern about it there is a good case for the development of health courses by teachers with special skills who would cooperate with concerned parents and provide sex education in schools tailored to the age and social development of the children and to the perspectives and language needs of different class, religious and ethnic groups; in certain religious schools, sex educaiton would necessarily be truncated to satisfy the school authorities. One point that must be emphasised is that sex education cannot be left until children reach senior school, for by that age a substantial minority of girls will have begun their periods. However, although there is a great deal to be done in order to develop worthwhile programmes, the first step is to recognise the need and to decide to take action to combat the basic ignorance about sexual matters found in all sections of society.

I have identified a number of problems in terms of provision of services. A crucial one is the treatment of men within the area of fertility. Over the past few years there have been great strides forward such as including men at the birth of their children. However, in some places men are still barred from antenatal care, and they have also been discouraged from attending birth control clinics on their own. In this respect we can welcome the Family Planning Association's 'Men Too' campaign in 1984/5. There is great scope for more adventurous action. I have had discussions with some of the agencies about the possibility of holding special sessions when they invite young men along for discussions, film shows, etc. This would be a useful development, for men in Britain have traditionally taken a large role in birth control practice. Even in this research we have seen that in the early experiences of intercourse men have been found more involved in taking precautions than women. The fact that they have lost this involvement at a later stage must pose questions about the nature of the services on offer.

Finally, in general terms I have found too much bureaucracy, with some of the simplest processes becoming mystified. We have seen that bureaucratic delays have made women wait unnecessarily for abortions and that regional disparities have produced inequality of access to free abortions. For most women, pregnancy tests are not available on the same day except from chemists shops, and these results are not acceptable within the health services – the tests have to be repeated to obtain services. This practice needs to be changed and same-day pregnancy tests should be provided on a routine basis. In terms of abortion, there should be an expansion of day care services to relieve pressure on hospital beds, to save money and to ensure that abortions are carried out earlier. Patients should be offered the choice of local or general anaesthetic and hopefully a higher percentage would avail themselves of local anaesthetic with its reduced risks. One innovation that could easily be introduced and that would help reduce the number of abortions would be the provision of after-sex birth control to couples using the condom as their main method of contraception. This would ensure that, if accidents occur in use, the couple are prepared and do not have to seek help urgently elsewhere when it may be inconvenient.

The providers in the National Health Service rightly expect the consumers to be efficient in their use of birth control. In return I would strongly argue that there is a need for the providers to set an example by improving their own efficiency and not keep people waiting for results or for urgent medical care. In all, while we can be heartened by the improvements since the mid-1960s, we must recognise that there is a long way to go before we can be happy with the quality of service offered.

5 Abortion Practice in the United States

Official data on abortion provision

Amidst great publicity and drama, abortion on request was legalised in New York State in 1970. As there was no residential requirement, abortion became legally available for any woman willing to travel. So, while there had been a variety of liberalising legislation, it is nevertheless convenient to use 1970 as a starting date for the collation of statistics.

The number and rate of abortions

The Centers for Disease Control reported 193,000 abortions in 1970, 485,000 in 1971 and 586,000 in 1972 (Tietze, 1983, p.33). There are good reasons for believing that these figures are in fact an underestimate: in 1973, the Centers for Disease Control produced an estimate of the number of abortions as 615,000 based on reports from Health Departments. Also in this year, the Alan Guttmacher Institute (AGI) began publishing data on the number of abortions based on information reported to it by abortion providers and its estimate for 1973 was 744,000. The AGI's data for 1973–81 are given in Table 5.1. The figures show a relatively large rate of increase until 1977 and that the number of abortions doubled between 1973 and 1979. However, since that time the abortion rate has remained relatively constant. One of the reasons for the increase was the fact that the AGI was getting more efficient in tracking down abortion providers. Henshaw *et al.*, who have taken over from Tietze in publishing the figures, suggest that their data are relatively accurate and that the few abortions missed out will be approximately balanced by a small amount of double counting (personal communication 1985). Another reason for the increase over the period was the decrease in illegal abortion.

Table 5.1 Number of abortions reported in the United States, 1973–1981

Year	Number	Rate per 1,000 women, 15–44	Ratio per 100 live births
1973	744,600	16.3	23.9
1974	898,600	19.3	28.2
1975	1,034,200	21.7	33.1
1976	1,179,300	24.2	36.1
1977	1,316,700	26.5	40.0
1978	1,409,600	27.7	41.3
1979	1,497,700	28.8	42.0
1980	1,553,900	29.3	42.8
1981	1,577,340	29.3	42.8

Sources: Tietze (1983) p.33; Henshaw, Binkin, Blaine and Smith (1985).
Note: Includes non-residents who had abortions in the USA.

In the USA as a whole the abortion rate is relatively high, with two abortions for every five births. There are nearly thirty abortions for every 1,000 women of childbearing age and two-thirds of these women (67.1 per cent) are having their first abortion. On the basis of these figures, more than four women out of ten will have an abortion some time in their lives. Seven out of ten seeking abortion were white and three out of ten were non-white (Henshaw, 1985). Further analysis of the racial characteristics of abortion patients is given later.

Women's demand for abortion is greater at the early ages. Table 5.2 shows that the rate of abortions per 1,000 in the age group increases with age until reaching a peak in the 18–19 group. In that cohort year nearly seven women in 100 will have an abortion. The rate remains at a relatively high level for those aged 20–24. However, for every five abortions in the 20–24 age group there are only three in the 25–29 group and less than two in the 30–34 group. The decline in the rate after the age of 25 may in large part be due to the increased percentage of women who become sterilised. The decline in abortion continues for the age group 35–39 in which less than one in 100 will have a termination in any one year.

If we use the alternative measure of comparing the ratio of abortions to the number of known conceptions, excluding

Table 5.2 Abortions by age: USA, 1981

Age	No. of abortions	Rate per 1,000	Ratio per 100 conceptions
under 15	15,240	8.6	43.6
15–17	175,930	30.1	42.2
18–19	257,400	61.8	40.3
20–24	554,940	51.1	30.3
25–29	316,260	31.4	22.0
30–34	167,240	17.7	23.9
35–39	69,510	9.5	35.6
40 +	20,820	3.4	51.3

Source: Henshaw, Binkin, Blaine and Smith (1985).
Note: The rate for the under-15 age group is based on the population of 14-year-old females, and for the 40+ age group on the population of women aged 40–44.

foetal spontaneous deaths, then we find a different pattern. The ratio is the highest at the two extremes. More than half the conceptions for women over the age of 40 end in abortion. Many of these women will have grown children and possibly grandchildren by this age, so they do not wish to return to having babies. The second highest ratio is for the under fifteens, closely followed by the 15–17 age group. At these early ages, those who do get pregnant often feel that they are not ready to care for a child adequately. The ratio of abortions then falls by about a half and in the 20–29-year-old group only one conception in five ends in abortion – the absolute number of abortions is high but it is in their twenties that the concentration of childbearing occurs. By the age group 30–34 the birth rate has fallen faster than the abortion rate, so the ratio of abortions to conception begins to rise again and in the 35–39 age group more than a third of conceptions are aborted.

Within the overall age groups a crucial factor is clearly the marital status of the woman. In 1981 less than one in ten of the conceptions for married women (9.1 per cent) ended in abortion, in contrast to nearly two-thirds of those for single women (64.8 per cent). Overall, the marital status of women seeking abortion for 1981 showed 18.9 per cent to be married. The rest were either single or widowed, divorced or separated.

Table 5.3 Abortions by number of living children: USA, 1981

No. of living children	No. of abortions	%
none	911,880	57.8
one	312,200	19.8
two	219,880	13.9
three	84,480	5.4
four	48,900	3.1
Total	1,577,340	100.0

Source: Henshaw, Binkin, Blaine and Smith (1985).

Another important factor is the number of children a woman already has. Table 5.3 shows that nearly six out of ten women seeking abortion had not had any children. The evidence of my research will suggest that the vast majority of these women will have families in due course. For many of them to have a baby at this stage in their lives would have forced them to live in inferior conditions and without the kind of support they would like to raise a child satisfactorily. One in five women had one child. In some cases they could be single parents but on other occasions families could feel the second pregnancy occurred too soon after the first. For many young couples the pleasure of having their first child conflicts with great financial problems. The mother may have to give up work and there will be hospital bills to pay and clothes, diapers, and other items to be bought. The parent(s) may be able to cope with one child but if it is followed too closely by a second pregnancy the problems can be compounded and people may feel they will not be able to look after both children properly. They may, for example, find that they would have to move to a larger home with extra rent or get a larger mortgage. This was the case with a young man of 23 who had a 6-month-old baby in 1985. He and his wife lived a long way from her parents and they felt that if they continued with the second pregnancy they would be in serious financial trouble. Furthermore, there was the question of whether the wife's health would suffer after having two children so close together. So they decided to have an abortion and planned to have their second child in the latter half of 1986.

The data show that only about one abortion in twelve (8.5 per cent) occurred to women with three or more children – in most cases presumably women who had completed their families. So, although fewer abortions occur to women with several children, in terms of influence on population size these are important. Abortion on young single women is not likely to have much effect on the population size. A few may not have children at all but on the other hand others may be able to have a greater number because they are able to choose to have them at a time when they can care for them properly.

Gestation

Table 5.4 shows that just over half of all abortions occur during the first eight weeks of gestation and nearly four out of five occur by 10 weeks. So the vast majority of abortions are carried out early in the pregnancy. One reason for this is that in large parts of the USA there are facilities for free same-day pregnancy testing. There will normally be counsellors on hand to discuss the implications of a pregnancy. Those who want to have abortions can arrange to have one in the next few days. Typically the woman will arrange to attend on a convenient day with a friend or her sexual partner. There will be both group and individual counselling sessions where the abortion operation is described and possible side-effects considered. Methods of birth control are also described. Before performing the abortion the doctor sees the woman alone to ensure that she is not being pressurised against her will. The operation itself takes about five minutes. The woman then moves to a recovery room where she is given coffee and biscuits; she is allowed to leave after there are seen to be no immediate contra-indications. The whole process usually takes about four or five hours.

None the less, nearly 9 per cent of abortions are carried out after the first trimester, and half of these are carried out after 16 weeks. There are many reasons for late abortion: some young women may not recognise the signs of pregnancy and at the other end of the age range women may assume that they have

Table 5.4 Gestation period and the number of abortions: USA, 1981

Weeks of gestation	No.	%
8 or below	810,300	51.4
9–10	423,910	26.9
11–12	203,970	12.9
13–15	75,770	4.8
16–20	49,600	3.1
21 +	13,790	0.9

Source: Henshaw, Binkin, Blaine and Smith (1985).

entered the change of life. In other cases a combination of factors operate to prevent the early detection of pregnancy. For example, a 24-year-old woman told me of her abortion four years earlier:

> After my first sex I only had it intermittently, one here one there. It wasn't until I got my first steady boyfriend that I realised that I'd better do something. I went to the College Infirmary and got a diaphragm. I was pretty good at using it but one time I didn't. I remember the night well. We were driving around with nothing to do when we decided to go to a motel. I didn't have my diaphragm with me. I was not in the habit of carrying it around. This was in the August and I went off to College. In the September I had a period as usual and I didn't have any sex for a few months so when my periods did not come I didn't think about it. I realised just before Christmas and I told the guy about it and he didn't want to know. He just wrote me a check for $300 but did not give me any support. Another friend of mine flew in to help and by the time I found someone to carry out the abortion it cost $1,400. I had saline it was very painful – worse than labour. You just want to die. You can't believe the pain . . . . [But] now I've no regrets. I've got my Bachelors from College and I intend to go back to school to become a psychologist.

Variations by state in the abortion rate

I have shown that the abortion rate in the United States is higher than in Britain. However, there are wide variations by state. Of the 1,577,340 abortions in 1981, an estimated 11,110 were obtained by non-residents of the United States. A further 6 per cent of residents had an abortion out of their own state. Table 5.5 gives the resident abortion rate by state per 1,000 women aged 15–44. It shows that the highest abortion rate by far was in Washington DC (which is co-extensive with the

Table 5.5 Number and rate of abortions by state: USA, 1981

State	No.	Rate	State	No.	Rate
Alabama	20,230	22.1	Missouri	23,460	20.8
Alaska	2,300	20.9	Montana	3,610	19.5
Arizona	16,350	25.0	Nebraska	5,630	15.8
Arkansas	7,890	15.4	Nevada	8,540	41.3
California	262,840	44.9	New Hampshire	4,990	22.2
Colorado	21,980	28.9	New Jersey	64,290	37.8
Connecticut	24,370	33.6	New Mexico	9,390	29.3
Delaware	4,030	30.8	New York	179,220	43.7
District of			North Carolina	32,970	23.1
Columbia	15,720	92.7	North Dakota	1,900	12.9
Florida	74,270	34.7	Ohio	59,710	23.7
Georgia	37,310	27.4	Oklahoma	12,600	17.9
Hawaii	8,760	37.1	Oregon	15,930	25.0
Idaho	3,490	15.8	Pennsylvania	64,860	24.4
Illinois	67,950	25.3	Rhode Island	6,030	29.2
Indiana	21,290	16.5	South Carolina	16,830	21.9
Iowa	9,620	14.7	South Dakota	1,880	12.4
Kansas	9,530	17.7	Tennessee	21,470	19.5
Kentucky	9,300	10.9	Texas	102,790	29.2
Louisiana	20,940	20.4	Utah	4,040	11.4
Maine	5,800	22.6	Vermont	3,170	25.4
Maryland	43,330	41.0	Virginia	39,440	29.5
Massachusetts	42,730	31.4	Washington S.	33,270	32.8
Michigan	64,120	29.1	West Virginia	5,270	12.1
Minnesota	17,900	18.4	Wisconsin	22,570	20.6
Mississippi	7,900	13.6	Wyoming	2,420	20.7
			Federal total	1,566,230	

Source: Henshaw (personal communication 1985).

District of Columbia), whose figure was more than three times the federal average (29.1). A number of factors are involved, including a disproportionate number of women in the age groups with high abortion rates such as students, and a high percentage of poor black women with higher than average abortion rates. Washington DC also has the highest proportion of non-residents having abortions: 49 per cent of the abortions carried out there are for women from other states. If a significant proportion of other non-residents were recorded as residents this could also be a partial explanation of the high rate in Washington DC. The second highest rate was in California, which had a rate less than half that recorded for DC. The Californian rate was closely followed by that of New York, Nevada and Maryland.

Several states had abortion rates less than half the federal average of 29.1 (residents only). The lowest rate was in Kentucky, where just over one woman in 100 had an abortion each year. The second lowest rate was in the Mormon stronghold of Utah and this was followed by West Virginia, South Dakota and North Dakota. Mississippi and Iowa were the other two states to have abortion rates below half the average.

So we can see that there are great regional variations. Even so, the rates on the whole are much higher than those for Britain. Scotland and Wales had lower abortion rates than any US state and England had a lower rate than all but four states.

The US survey sample

Characteristics of the sample

It is instructive to compare my US sample with the latest national data (1981) in terms of age, marital status and race. I should point out that the AGI data are two years older than the bulk of my information.

Table 5.6 shows some of the essential features in terms of age of my sample in the United States compared with the national data. In both samples, the largest group was the age range 20–24. In my sample nearly two in five were in this category,

Table 5.6 Comparison of age structure of survey sample with national data

Age	Survey sample No.	%	National (1981) %
under 18	94	8.3	12.2
18–19	203	18.0	16.3
20–24	445	39.4	35.2
25–29	222	19.7	20.0
30–34	103	9.1	10.6
35 +	48	4.2	5.7
not known	14	1.2	—
Total	1,129	100.0	100.0

Source: Henshaw, Binkin, Blaine and Smith (1985) and this survey.

which is a slight over-representation compared to the national data. Nearly 29 per cent were in the two age ranges 25–29 and 30–34 in my sample, which is in proportion to the national data (nearly 31 per cent). My sample was slightly under-represented at the ends of the age range. So it could be that my sampling points had a lower proportion of the very young and those over the age of 35 compared to the proportions of abortions carried out nationally. However, such differences are not great, and overall my age structure is broadly in line with what would be expected.

This also applied to marital status. Table 5.7 shows that less than one in five (17.2 per cent) of the sample were married at the time of the abortion. This is similar to the results obtained from the national data. Of those women who were not married, more than two-thirds were single (67.9 per cent) and just over one in eight (13.3 per cent) were widowed, divorced or separated (W/D/S). The 150 women who made up the W/D/S group consisted of 97 who were divorced, 41 who were separated and only 12 who were widowed.

The racial characteristics of the sample were obtained by asking the women: 'In which of the following racial groups would you place yourself?' A list was given and the results are tabulated in Table 5.8. They show that 72 per cent of my sample were white, compared to 70.2 per cent of the national

Table 5.7 Comparison of marital status of survey sample with national data

Status	Survey sample No.	%	National (1981) %
married	194	17.2	18.9
single	767	67.9	
widowed/divorced/ separated	150	13.3	81.1
not known	18	1.6	
Total	1,129	100.0	100.0

Source: Henshaw, Binkin, Blaine and Smith (1985) and this survey.

Table 5.8 Comparison of racial characteristics of survey sample with national data

Grouping	Survey sample No.	%		National (1981) %
white	814	72.1		70.2
black	145	12.9		
Asian	31	2.7		
Hispanic	97	8.6	non-white	29.8
other	27	2.4		
not known	15	1.3		
Total	1,129	100.0		100.0

Source: Henshaw, Binkin, Blaine and Smith (1985) and this survey.

data. Of the non-whites, the highest percentage were blacks, who made up just over one in eight of the total sample. A further one in twelve were Hispanic and 2.7 per cent were Asian. However, the Asian group seems to be largely made up of people of Chinese origin than from the Indian subcontinent, as is the case in Britain. 'Other' categories included American Indians.

The religious beliefs of the sample were determined by asking people the question 'What is your religious preference?' Table 5.9 shows that more than two in five of the respondents

Table 5.9 Religious characteristics of survey sample

Religion	No.	%
Catholic	466	41.3
Protestant	363	32.2
Jewish	24	2.1
Muslim/Hindu	4	0.3
not known/none	272	24.1
Total	1,129	100.0

were Catholic. In contrast to our findings in Britain, this is much above the percentage of Catholics in the population. (Although there are no national data on religion, surveys usually find that about a quarter of US citizens are Catholic.) The reasons for this are not clear. In part it may be due to the fact that I sampled disproportionately in Catholic areas. However, against this I must say that whenever I have sampled in the United States I have come up with a disproportionate number of Catholics. In 1981, the *Boston Globe* (8 and 9 January) reported data from my surveys showing more Catholics in abortion clinics in Boston and Long Island than might have been expected. The results were attacked by the Archdiocese and even after I was back in London the controversy continued. Patricia McCormack, the Health Editor for UPI, was quoted:

A study reporting two thirds of the patients at three abortion clinics in Boston and New York state were Catholic still has church leaders angered – five weeks after its publication . . . . Church leaders continue to angrily dispute the accuracy of the report, even though its findings follow a pattern similar to earlier studies. The controversy was touched off by a report published last month that two thirds of the 1,162 abortion patients at a Boston clinic and facilities in Hempstead and Happauge on Long Island, N.Y. between 1978 and 1980 were Catholic. In his report Dr. Colin Francome said 66% of the patients were Catholic 'Whereas the overall population of Boston is only 35 per cent Catholic'. Peter Conley, a spokesman for the Boston Archdiocese, claimed that one inaccuracy is that actually 64% of Boston's population – not 35% – are Catholic. [*Mesabi News*, 16 February 1981]

Conley may be right that the area immediately surrounding the clinic had a higher proportion of Catholics than the whole of the Archdiocese. However, that could not be the explanation in the clinic in Hempstead, New York, for that found a similar disproportionate number of Catholics, despite the fact it was in a black area.

Results of the Survey

Sex education   The survey began its questions about sexuality with a simple question about the source of first information about menstruation. This was to give some information about the pattern of sex education and also a bottom line indicator about the level of information: if women were not being properly informed about such a basic matter it was clearly a matter of some concern and a bad omen for the general level of sex education in the society. The respondents were asked: 'When you had your first menstrual period, had anyone told you what to expect?' The replies are given in Table 5.10. If the information from non-respondents is redistributed in proportion, then just over three women out of five were given the information by their mother (62.8 per cent). For coding purposes this included the few who had replied with such comments as 'mother and others' or 'mother and school'. Less than one in 200 had received the first information from their father, which reveals a clear sexual segregation in the dissemination of such information. However, by far the most surprising finding is that beteen one in four and one in five (23 per cent) had replied 'no one'. This raises important issues about the role of the parents and the schools in terms of sex education. Many parents seem to think schools inform children on sexual matters, whereas for many children the information is not provided by anyone.

In the chapter on Britain I suggested that one of the more understandable reasons for not giving information about the onset of periods was if it occurred at an early age. The age of

Table 5.10   Source of first information about menstruation

Source	No.	%	Corrected %
mother	638	56.5	62.8
father	4	0.4	0.4
friend	23	2.0	2.3
teacher	64	5.7	6.3
sibling	36	3.2	3.5
relative	12	1.1	1.2
doctor	5	0.4	0.5
no one	233	20.6	23.0
not known	114	10.2	
Total	1,129	100.0	100.0

Table 5.11   Age at commencement of periods

Age	No.	%
under 11	34	3.0
11	186	16.5
12	260	23.0
13	343	30.4
14	167	14.8
15	73	6.5
16	35	3.1
17	12	1.1
18	2	0.2
not known	17	1.5
Total	1,129	100.0

menarche in the US sample is shown in Table 5.11. One in five of those responding had their first period *before* they were 12. This indicates clearly the need to ensure that this basic information is provided at an early age. Some families are making it the practice to discuss sex openly with their children from the very beginning, and this has certain virtues although there is still the problem as to what the child can absorb at each age. Children sometimes find birth control appliances, and their questions can result in parents having to answer questions unexpectedly; even some of the most liberal people can face embarrassing moments. For example, a 27-year-old mother told me of her experience with her 3-year-old son:

> Yesterday he found a condom that was left by the bed and he was playing with it. He opened it and asked me what it was. I told him it was Daddy's and he kept going on about it saying 'Why, Why'?, you know the kind of things kids do. Then I said Daddy puts it on his penis. Then he kept going on saying: 'Why? Do you wear one? Why haven't I got one?' Then I said, 'It's to stop us having any more babies'. Then I tried to divert the conversation because I was feeling quite uncomfortable. I said we wouldn't want more babies because: 'I wouldn't be able to spend as much time with you.'
>
> I thought it was OK we were talking about what it was like to have a new baby. I thought the conversation was ended. I was in the bathroom and he went in to see Judy the nanny and he was carrying one of these condoms. She snatched it away from him and said: 'Where did you get that?' She said 'It's rubbish!' He said 'No it's not, it's what Daddy wears on his penis to stop having any more babies.' At which stage she got very shocked and said 'Who told you that? Who did you hear that from?' When he said 'Mommy', you can imagine I was very embarrassed.

The mother suggested to me afterwards that she thought she could have dealt with it a little differently and not gone into such anatomical detail, which such a young child could clearly not comprehend. Other people have told me of similar experiences of being surprised by questions and not knowing at what level to pitch their answers. So there seems to be a need to make some basic information available about how to deal with situations that are likely to arise so that parents can be prepared to answer their children honestly but at a level that the child can understand.

First intercourse   The questionnaire asked about age at the time of first intercourse. Table 5.12 shows that one in five of the sample had their first intercourse at the age of 15 or under. Furthermore, a total of three in five had their first intercourse

Table 5.12   Age at first intercourse

Age	No.	%	Corrected %
15 or under	226	20.4	20.3
16–17	442	39.2	39.8
18–19	310	26.8	27.9
20–24	125	11.3	11.2
25–29	7	0.6	0.6
30–34	2	0.2	0.2
not known	17	1.4	
Total	1,129	100.0	100.0

by the age of 17. It seems that women in the United States had begun their sexual activity at an earlier age than their British counterparts. (Further discussion of this will occur in the next chapter.) About one in eight of the sample began their first intercourse after the age of 20, which is about one in six of those who had reached this age.

Many people I interviewed started their sex lives with virtually no knowledge about what was going to occur. For example, a 24-year-old woman living in Washington DC told me in February 1985:

> My mother told me about my periods but not about sex. I was seventeen at the time and I knew nothing about it. I had no idea what to expect. I did not know that a man ejaculated. I didn't know it was going to be so painful. I knew nothing about getting pregnant. I knew it was possible but I didn't know how. I didn't use any birth control myself for four years, during which time my partners used withdrawal or condoms. Once my mother realised I was having sex she told me about birth control. I went to the woman's pavilion and got a diaphragm from a woman gynaecologist.

In view of such findings it is less than surprising that those involved had little knowledge of birth control. One factor that might affect birth control use is the woman's relationship with her partner at first intercourse. Table 5.13 shows that in almost two-thirds of the cases the first intercourse was with a steady boyfriend. The rest were relatively evenly divided between

Table 5.13   Relationship with partner at first intercourse

Relationship	No.	%
casual	178	15.8
steady	706	62.6
fiancé/husband to be	176	15.6
other	21	1.9
husband	24	2.1
not known	24	2.1
Total	1,129	100.0

casual boyfriend and fiancé/husband to be. Very few of the 344 ever married women had their first intercourse with their husbands.

Some states have been trying to force children to talk to their parents about abortion and birth control. One problem with this is the gap between the generations in terms of passing information and the possible teenage conflicts. An illustrative example was the daughter of a wealthy lawyer. She told me she was having some conflicts with her parents and that she was into drugs at the ages of 12 and 13. She had her first sex to annoy her parents. Just before her thirteenth birthday she had intercourse with a 20-year-old friend who her father had introduced to her. She pretended she was experienced and afterwards he told her that he would not have had sex if he had known she was a virgin. They did not use any birth control and she did not get any protection until she was seventeen. In this case and some others there was a big gap between the parents and the children in terms of sexuality. The woman, who has now married and has a child of her own, told me that when she was living with her parents sex was something that was always avoided in the household. Nobody ever saw other members of the family undressed and it was as if the subject was one big secret. This parent/child division is a topic to which I shall return in subsequent chapters.

Birth control use at first intercourse   On the question of birth control usage, I was able to compare the replies of my sample with the results of a national survey carried out in 1982 (see

Table 5.14 Birth control use at first intercourse

Method	Sample survey No.	%	National (1981) %
pill	190	16.8	12.6
IUD	2	0.2	0.2
diaphragm (cap)	43	3.8	0.8
sheath	205	18.2	17.1
withdrawal	149	13.2	8.5
safe period	53	4.7	2.4
suppository	19	1.7 } other	2.9
foam	52	4.6 }	
not using/not known	416	36.8	55.5
Total	1,129	100.0	100.0

Source: Data derived from Pratt *et al.* (1984) p.19, and this survey.
Note: National data are for women aged 15–44.

Table 5.14). The results from my survey show that the most common method of birth control at first intercourse was the sheath, but even this was used by less than one in five couples. If the percentage of those using withdrawal is added, we can see that just under a third of couples were using male methods (31.4 per cent). The most popular female method was the pill, which was used by one in six (16.8 per cent). Overall just under a third (31.8) per cent used female methods. The rest did not use anything. Of course, a small minority of these respondents may in fact have been hoping to become pregnant.

The national data show several differences from my figures. The first is that my sample of abortion patients was more likely to use birth control at first intercourse. There are at least two possible explanations for this. First of all, my sample was much younger than the national 15–44 age group and so if birth control practices had shown improvement over the previous twenty years this would have been reflected in my data showing a higher degree of usage. A more important reason is that many women in the national sample were married before they began having intercourse and so may not have used birth control because they were preparing to start a family. Of those women married between 1975 and 1982, one in five reported that they did not have intercourse before marriage. Those in the sample married before that date were even more likely to marry as virgins. Furthermore, there may have been others who, while they were not married, were about to be so and so were not too concerned about their birth control usage.

Just under one in five couples used condoms at first intercourse, but many stopped using them as soon as possible. One man told me he had his first sex at the age of 21. He said:

> Our first sex was planned. I'd delayed it and delayed it as I didn't want to pressure her into nothing and waited until she was ready to come naturally. For a while we had some foreplay and then backing off. When we first had sex I used trojans and she used something [pessary]. I didn't like trojans, I didn't like the way they felt so sometimes I withdrew depending on the time of the month.

Others, however, used condoms as their regular method of birth control. Thus, a 19-year-old student, interviewed in February 1985 when he was attending an abortion clinic with his girlfriend, told me that he used the condom 'every single time' and that the pregnancy must have resulted from a malfunction. He thought the problem may have been due to the fact that he had bought cheaper condoms rather than one of the more expensive brands. Regular users of the condom nevertheless seem rare. In my discussions with young men I found that some of them had stopped using condoms not because they had found them uncomfortable but rather because their partners did. Indeed, one fact that surprised me in interviews was the number of occasions that women objected to the condom. A 20-year-old Jewish woman told me that she had her first sex at the age of 17 after dating for nine months. She did not use birth control and only once did her partner use a condom. She commented with an air of finality: 'That was the last time I used it in my whole life.' On my probing the reasons for her hostility, she said 'I hate them. They take away some of the feeling. They feel rubbery. Have you ever heard the expression "It's like swimming with your boots on"?'

Communication on sexual matters   I asked respondents about the people they had had discussions with about birth control. Table

Table 5.15 People with whom the sample had discussed birth control

Relationship	No.	%
no one	45	4.5
father	45	4.5
mother	361	36.3
brother	51	5.1
sister	327	32.8
girlfriend	585	58.8
teacher	39	3.9
partner	727	73.1
other	85	8.6

Note: Non-respondents excluded.

5.15 shows that only one in twenty had not discussed birth control with anyone. Three-quarters had talked about it with their partners, and nearly three in five had discussed it with a girlfriend. There seems to have been relatively little family discussion. Only just over a third discussed it with their mother and only one in twenty with their father. This is scarcely surprising given the significant minority of parents who do not even give their daughters essential information about the menstrual cycle. Of course, for those parents who oppose their children's sexuality the discussion of birth control might be seen as condoning their children's behaviour. A 19-year-old Catholic told me she learned about her menstrual cycle in school and that her mother did not tell her anything: 'I come from a strict Catholic family so they kept sex under wraps.' It seems that in many families the subject of sex cannot be dealt with on a rational basis. I asked a number of the people what happened in the family if a sex programme appeared on the television when they were all together. In many cases the young people said there would be great discomfort and sometimes they reported that their mother would leave the room. My interviews with young men also indicated that it was rare to find parental discussion. One exception was a 21 year old who said that his mother had told him about sex when he was 17 or 18 but that she didn't tell him anything nice about it, just the mechanics of it.

Although the percentage discussing birth control with their mothers was small, the number discussing it with their fathers was minute. Only one in twenty did so, which is one-eighth of the number who discussed it with their mother. This sex difference was also evident amongst siblings: women in the sample were six times as likely to discuss sex with their sisters as with their brothers. In all, nearly one-third discussed it with their sisters.

There also seems to have been little education in schools on the matter of birth control. Less than one in twenty-five of the total sample said they had discussed birth control with a teacher. At face value it would seem to indicate little teaching of sex education in the schools, although some people reported seeing films. It thus seems that there is a lack of knowledge that in many cases could lead to unwanted pregnancies. Lesley, a counsellor for a number of years, told me:

> There is a general ignorance. Many women who come here have no idea of their anatomy. I had a little girl fifteen years called me over. She said the reason she became pregnant was because she had an orgasm. Her boyfriend had told her that if she had an orgasm she could become pregnant and it was her first one. Another young girl told me her boyfriend was a miracle baby. He was the seventh son and the seventh son was always sterile. She refused birth control because she said it could never happen again.

Lesley went on to comment: 'I think people are ashamed of their bodies and they are ashamed of having sex. I think we need to say "You are going to have sex, let's be responsible about it".' This is, of course, a view that encounters a great deal of opposition from those who feel sex education leads to promiscuity. Other counsellors have also told me of bizarre beliefs. One of the more unusual was a 16-year-old young lady who said that she did not want the Copper 7 because if she was caught in lightning she might be struck by it. Many counsellors have remarked on the general belief that a person could only have three abortions and then would be sterile. One told me that she dealt with that view at least once a day.

The questionnaire also asked women about discussion of the pregnancy. Table 5.16 shows that the people told about the

Table 5.16 People with whom the sample had discussed the pregnancy

Relationship	No.	%
father	67	6.7
mother	187	18.7
no one	70	7.0
brother	57	5.7
sister	180	18.0
girlfriend	477	47.7
partner	726	72.6
other	81	8.1

Note: Non-respondents excluded.

pregnancy were very similar to those with whom the women had had discussions about birth control. So more than seven out of ten had told their partner and nearly half had discussed the pregnancy with a girlfriend. However, less than one in five told their mother. Those who did were very often those needing help and were more inclined to be the younger women. The older women were less likely to tell their mother of this kind of personal problem. Within the family, mothers and sisters were much more likely to be informed than fathers and brothers.

Those not telling their parents often reported that they wanted to protect them. A 24-year-old single woman living at home told me about her abortion some years previously:

> I would rather die than them find out. I love them so dearly I would never want to hurt them. They have been too good to me. If they had found out it would have changed our relationship in the long term. I can talk about general sex to them but not personal experiences. They are liberal but not with their own children. Part of my happiness is keeping them happy.

This kind of feeling seems to be even more prevalent among those who have moved away from the family home.

It is relatively unusual for mothers to attend abortion clinics with their daughters, but I did interview one such couple.

Table 5.17 Birth control use at conception

Use	No.	%	Corrected %
thinking of using	124	11.0	12.7
sometimes using	309	27.4	31.7
always using	242	21.4	24.9
not using	299	26.5	30.7
not known	155	13.7	
Total	1,129	100.0	100.0

Although they were both practising Catholics, the mother told me: 'Women's bodies are their own, I don't care what the Church says.' She found out about her 18-year-old daughter's possibly pregnancy because she monitored her periods. She said: 'I kept on her case. I asked her whether she had come on yet and made her go for tests. So far two have been negative and two positive and so we don't know yet.' She went on to say that she was very disappointed, especially as the daughter had already had one abortion. However, she supported her daughter because she felt that a baby at her age would ruin her life.

Birth control use at conception Respondents were asked about their birth control use at conception. Table 5.17 shows that, of those responding to the question, only one in four were always using a method of birth control. Three out of ten (31.7 per cent) were using it sometimes, but more than two in five (43.4 per cent) were not using it at all.

Non-use of birth control Those not using birth control sometimes complained about the lack of choice:

IUD too dangerous, other methods not spontaneous, pill too many side effects – careless. [19-year-old single white woman from Massachusetts]

I would like to know what kind of contraception I can use. I cannot use the IUD or the birth control pill.

Did not think something were good for you. [19-year-old black woman]

Table 5.18   Reasons for not using birth control

Reason	No.	% of respondents
thought sterile	47	7.1
had intercourse unexpectedly	318	48.3
cost	29	4.4
did not know of any	8	1.2
did not know where to go	26	3.9
intended to use but had not made an appointment	154	23.4
religion says wrong	13	2.0
stopped using because of side effects	176	26.7
hoped pregnancy would lead to marriage	1	0.2
did not intend to have intercourse anymore	45	6.8

Note: Calculations based on 659 respondents. Non-respondents and those pregnant through birth control failure excluded. Percentages add to more than 100 owing to multiple responses.

Some seemed to have a fear of birth control. A 17-year-old black woman said: 'I was scared to get it', and this kind of comment suggests the need for better education.

In order to analyse non-use further, I gave a checklist. The results are tabulated in Table 5.18 and show that nearly half of those who did not use birth control said that they had had intercourse unexpectedly. Very often it is those who do not really want to accept their sexuality who are most at risk. A young 'born again' Christian couple I interviewed in New York typify the problem. They took the view that they should not have sex before marriage but found that sometimes 'the spirit was willing but the flesh was weak'. In the year prior to my interview they had had an abortion. This time the young man had been away at college and come home for the weekend unexpectedly. His girlfriend and he were so pleased to see each other that one thing led to another and she was back for a second abortion. I asked him whether they were planning to continue with this ideal of chastity and occasional failures and he seemed to think they would. However, when she came away from the doctor she had received a supply of pills. Others had written such things as: 'It was unexpected, one of those things and with the condom it doesn't feel right.'

The second largest category was of those who had stopped taking the pill. Typical comments written on the questionnaire were:

> Pills make me sick and I can't do my job. [23-year-old single black woman]

> I had been on the pill and had no problems for 4 years, but people were telling me bad things about it. After being so used to it, it is really hard to change to have to think about birth control. I got pregnant only 1½ months after I came off the pill. [24-year-old single white woman from California]

> Ran out of pill and hadn't gotten a refill. [20-year-old from Louisiana]

> I heard the pill gives you cancer and a lot of things and with everything else you still come out pregnant. [18-year-old Mexican American]

> I had forgotten – was about to start again in a few weeks but was too late. [20-year-old white woman]

One of the problems seems to be that the pill is so closely identified as the method of birth control that if they did not use it they often did not get an alternative.

The third biggest reason for non-use was the failure to make an appointment. A 20-year-old male, who was accompanying his 17-year-old girlfriend, told me: 'We weren't using anything. We talked about it. Last year I was going with a girl and she got pregnant but had a miscarriage. I've been with this one for three months and we discussed it but we did not get our act together.'

An unexpectedly high number thought that either they or their partner were sterile. A 33-year-old woman from California wrote: 'Had not used birth control for the last five years as I was unable to get pregnant when trying to conceive.' A 35-year-old divorced 'limo' driver commented: 'Thought I was non fertile.' A single 16 year old in California wrote: 'Thought boyfriend was sterile.' Presumably this was becuase he had had sex before and not made his partner pregnant. In a number of cases the women were deceived. A separated 24 year old commented: 'He supposedly had a vasectomy.' Another from New York said: 'Yes, never think your partner is sterile.'

One of the respondents, a 25-year-old Catholic woman whose husband had had a vasectomy, became pregnant as the result of rape. She commented: 'Thanks to your services we can get rid of unwanted pregnancies.' So there were a variety of reasons for non-use.

Birth control failure Those who became pregnant through failure of method often felt somewhat let down. Table 5.19 compares the failure rates of various birth control methods in my study with the nationwide usage rates by all women aged 15–44 in the period 1973–82 (as reported by Bachrach, 1984). The data show that the highest percentage of birth control failures (21 per cent) occurred among users of the diaphragm. This is more than twice the proportion of women in the fertile age range using the diaphragm. However, when account is taken of the fact that a high percentage of abortion patients are single women, the diaphragm does not fare so badly: 13.5 per

Tale 5.19 Pregnancy because of birth control failure

Method of birth control	No. of failures	%	Nationwide usage of method (1973–82) %
pill	65	16.6	28.6
IUD	8	2.0	7.3
cap (diaphragm)	82	20.9	8.3
sheath	72	18.3	12.2
withdrawal	56	14.2	2.0
safe period	38	9.7	4.0
suppository	21	5.3	2.5★
foam	51	13.0	2.4
sterilisation	—	—	32.7
Total	393	100.0	100.0

Sources: Bachrach (1984) p.254 (Nationwide data for all women aged 15–44) and this survey.
Note: Non-respondents excluded. ★ includes all other methods.

cent of single women use it, so its 20.9 per cent failure rate is not that much of an over-representation. The sheath also comes out fairly well in terms of effectiveness: 12.2 per cent used this method and it resulted in 18.3 per cent of the failures. When account is taken of the fact that nationally a third of the women are sterilised, the condom is hardly over-represented at all. A 27-year-old Californian woman commented about her condom failure: 'Even tho' I feel a fool to have used methods that failed when more evidently effective ways were available – if I'd had to continue the pregnancy I think my life would have been ruined; an unwanted child etc.'

In contrast, withdrawal did not seem to fare very well as a birth control method. It is seven times over-represented in terms of its overall usage, and nearly five times when patient characteristics and sterilisation are taken into account. This degree of over-representation suggests that those who practise withdrawal are either not very skilled or are rather casual. A 27-year-old archeologist wrote simply: 'He forgot to withdraw.' A 20-year-old white woman said she became pregnant through the failure of withdrawal when she was about to go on the pill. However, she then commented: 'I do not consider withdrawal to be a contraceptive. We considered there to be no risk due to no sperm being produced – evidently there must have been "seepage" when I was fertile.'

The safe period is used by 4.0 per cent of women nationwide, but accounted for one case in ten of birth control failure. This may have been through inaccuracy because of the dates and even those using the mucus analysis can have problems: 'I have studied fertility awareness and I had checked my mucus that day or morning. But intercourse took place at 3 a.m. or so and my fertility could easily have changed during all those hours – it was also unexpected.'

The pill is under-represented (accounting for one in six cases of method failure), especially when we take into account the fact that over half the single women in the United States are using it as their method of birth control. The failure of the pill was usually accompanied by some problems with the user. A 24-year-old black woman commented: 'I was told when you miss a pill to double up. Now I am going to think for myself and use the pill and the diaphragm when I forget the pill.'

The IUD was also under-represented, constituting only one in fifty (2.0 per cent) of the failures, However, it is a relatively minor method and more so amongst the single, of whom only 5.5 per cent use it. We do know of course that it is possible to become pregnant with an IUD in place. A 26-year-old divorced white woman reported: 'My personal Ob/gyn attempted to remove IUD but was unsuccessful. I do have copies of X rays taken that day with me for reference.'

Repeat abortions In my sample, nearly two in five women (39.6 per cent) were having a repeat abortion. This is slightly higher than the figure in the data published by the Alan Guttmacher Institute (35.1 per cent), but the difference is not great (Henshaw *et al.*, 1985).

The number of repeat abortions raises many issues and questions. Some people take the view that repeated abortions lead to possible sterility and the increased likelihood of miscarariage. Others point out the 'irresponsibility' of those who have repeat abortions. However, some of those working within the general field of child care, while not taking a light view of abortion, consider that it is better that those who are irresponsible should have abortions rather than bring children into the world who they will not look after properly.

Table 5.20   Repeat abortions and age at first intercourse

| Age at first intercourse | Previous abortions | | | |
	None %	One %	Two %	Three %
13 or under	3.0	2.6	8.2	4.4
14–15	15.7	18.7	24.7	13.3
16–17	37.4	43.5	38.9	53.3
18–19	30.8	25.0	18.8	22.2
20–24	12.1	9.5	9.4	6.8
25 +	1.0	0.7		
Total	100.0	100.0	100.0	100.0
Number	624	304	85	45

Note: Non-respondents to questions on repeat abortions or age at first intercourse excluded.

One question that is raised is whether those having repeat abortions were relatively young when they began having intercourse. The results are tabulated in Table 5.20, which shows some evidence that the abortion repeaters began their intercourse at an earlier age, but the results are confusing. The percentage of those who had had their first intercourse below the age of 16 rose from 18.7 per cent for those having their first abortion to 21.3 per cent of those having their second abortion and 32.9 per cent of those having their third abortion. However, the forty-five women in the sample who were in for their fourth or subsequent abortion do not show this pattern. In fact, they were less likely than even the women having their first abortion to have had their first sex under the age of 16.

A second question is whether those who have had repeat abortions have had a history of non-use of birth control. It is therefore instructive to compare the groupings in terms of their use of birth control when they started having intercourse. The results are given in Table 5.21. Here again the evidence does not show that those with several abortions were less likely to use birth control when they started having intercourse. In fact, the reverse is the case. The women who were in for their first abortion were the least likely to have used birth control at first intercourse, whereas those with three or more abortions were the most likely to have used it.

This finding was confirmed by the data on birth control use at the time of conception (see Table 5.22). These suggest that

Table 5.21 Repeat abortions and birth control use at first abortion

Birth control use at first intercourse	Previous abortions							
	None		One		Two		Three	
	No.	%	No.	%	No.	%	No.	%
male method	196	35.1	98	36.3	27	36.5	16	41.0
female method	203	36.4	98	36.3	27	36.5	17	43.6
none	159	28.5	74	27.4	20	27.0	6	15.4
Total	558	100.0	270	100.0	74	100.0	39	100.0

Note: Non-respondents to questions on repeat abortions or birth control use excluded.

Table 5.22 Repeat abortions and birth control use at conception

Birth control use at conception	Previous abortions							
	None		One		Two		Three	
	no.	%	no.	%	no.	%	no.	%
none	201	36.0	60	22.0	21	29.6	13	33.3
thinking of it	78	14.0	31	11.4	10	14.1	2	5.1
sometimes	155	27.8	103	37.7	23	32.4	13	33.3
always using	124	22.2	79	28.9	17	23.9	11	28.3
Total	558	100.0	273	100.0	71	100.0	39	100.0

Note: Non-respondents to questions on repeat abortions or birth control use excluded.

those who are in for repeat abortions have been more assiduous in birth control usage. It is none the less surprising that only one in four of the women who were having their third or subsequent abortion were always using birth control.

One fact that surprised me was that women having multiple abortions may still not agree with the operation in principle. Thus, a 27-year-old black woman from Louisiana set out her position:

> I am really against abortion until I had to have one. I have had three abortions. I will never have another. I would advise anyone not to have one. Ask questions and be more careful before you get involved, see Planned Parenthood for your sake and the baby.

Others have no such conflicts. An 18-year-old woman I interviewed presenting for her second abortion had her first abortion at 15 after having sex only once. She felt it was necessary for her life to develop and that she could not look after a child at her present age, let alone three years earlier. Her mother knew about this abortion and was very disappointed, but she had forgotten to take the pill a few times. She very much hoped to have children when she was older.

Very often those women having their second abortion had had one when they were much younger and may have had a child in the meantime. This was the case with a 25 year old who had had a very difficult family life and left home at the age of sixteen. Her parents had split up and for a time she lived on social security. In her teens she became pregnant while using the condom and had an abortion. She then married and had two children who were aged 3 and nearly 1. She had now become pregnant once more, this time on the diaphragm and felt it may have been due to the fact that she lost a great deal of weight while breastfeeding the baby. She had only stopped nursing for a short time before becoming pregnant. Her husband agreed with her that this pregnancy was bad timing. The fact that they had little family support meant that he looked after the children while she worked and vice versa. She commented: 'We are working a juggling act and it couldn't work with three.' She also mentioned the fact that they could not live without her money and in any case she did not want to spend the summer season when she would be earning her money 'gavroned out'. She said that she had no regrets about her abortions. They were due to bad timing. In answer to my question about her religious feeling she said she was a Catholic and did go to church. However, she clearly did not agree with the Church on the question of fertility control. She said 'They are not the ones who have to raise it. Interest rates are out of this world. We have to know that we can bring up our children properly.'

A second woman had a similar experience. At the time of the interview in 1984 she was 24. Her first abortion occurred at the age of 20. At the time she had been under some stress about losing her job and her relationship had been suffering some strain. In the month she became pregnant she had intercourse with two men and did not know who caused the pregnancy. After long discussions with her main partner and friends she decided there was no alternative to an abortion. This led to them engaging in some serious thinking about their relationship. They decided that they wanted to have a child and within two months she was pregnant again. This time there were no complications about the likely fatherhood, they were married and she had a son. Within nine months she was pregnant again and, although the couple felt it was going to be difficult looking after two children under the age of 2, they continued the pregnancy and had a second son. This put them under a great deal of financial strain as they had to move house and face a large mortgage, but they had help from the grandparents in terms of both finance and babysitting. However, when the youngest son was just over 1 year she became pregnant for the fourth time. They had been using a combination of the diaphragm and the condom alternately but on some occasions around the time of the period had not been using anything. She thought that the reason for the pregnancy was that she had miscalculated the dates. Since that time the couple have been much more regular in their birth control use. They are in the process of deciding whether to have a third child. She told me: 'I would dearly love a little girl. I'd love to put her in dresses. I love the boys but there is something about a girl. One thing is I would love her to have a baby. I think it really would be a wonderful thing to watch your own daughter have a baby.' She went on to say that she would make some decision in the next few years. If there were to be another pregnancy, she wanted to be certain that she was financially secure so that she could enjoy it without incessant concern about money.

So we can see that these women have felt abortion to be the right decision for them for various reasons at different stages of their life.

The highest number of abortions reported in my survey was seven. However, during the course of the observation for this research I came across a 30-year-old woman in New York State who had had eight. I first met her in 1977 after five abortions and she had a further three in seven years. I asked her whether she was irresponsible in her birth control practice and she said that on only three of the occasions was she not using anything and one of these cases was rape. I asked her to go over her history and she told me (prompts omitted):

I was twelve when I had my first sex. It was with a casual boyfriend and I just wanted to get it over with. I just thought 'I don't want to be a virgin anymore'. . . . It wasn't painful and we didn't use any birth control method. . . . He was about 19 or 20. . . My first abortion was at the age of 15 at a hospital . . . No I'd not been using any contraception and I'd been fucking like a rabbit. I didn't learn anything about birth control at home or at school. My parents are Catholic and very strict they didn't think I should have sex.

They found out about the abortion and came with me to see the doctor afterwards. He asked me if I wanted to go on the pill with my parents in the room. Of course I said 'No'. I could have killed him. My parents thought it was going to be my one and only time. Of course I got pregnant again. This time they said I must go on birth control, they said I had no choice. For two years I was on the pill and I was O.K. But then I got cystitis and went off the pill. I got on the coil. It had no copper in it and I got pregnant with it in position. Then I got a Copper 7 and after a year got pregnant again. I had another Copper 7 and for two years nothing. Next after that I got discomfort. I tried the diaphragm but got pregnant on that. That may have been the weight thing. Then it was rape. I was actually attacked twice. The first time was more traumatic. I was walking home and a jogger went by the opposite way. He asked directions and I gave him information. Then he came up behind me and put his hands round my throat. We were laying on the ground when a car drove by. I kicked him in the balls and ran and banged on a door and an old man answered. He drove me home and I reported it to the police but nothing happened. The next time I was actually raped. I was with a friend I had casually dated for a year when I got ill drinking vodka and grapefruit. I was sick for four hours and woke up with this guy humping me. I was so pissed off but didn't report it to the police. I asked him to come for the abortion. I rang him up at home but they said he had gone away.

She was 24 at the time of this her sixth abortion. For the next four years she had been on the diaphragm but had abortions at the ages of 26 and 29. She commented on her birth control failures: 'I use extra cream so it's coming out but it doesn't matter. I'm tempted to go back on the pill. My doctor says I could.'

I asked her whether she wanted children and she said she would love to have them if she could meet the right man. Over the years I knew she had had some traumatic relationships and I asked her how things were at present. She told me she had a wonderfully nice young man. He was four years younger than her and 'really cute'. A few days later she introduced him to me

Table 5.23   Repeat abortions and ethnic groups

	Black		Hispanic		White	
first abortion	75	54.8	49	55.7	464	59.6
second abortion	40	29.2	27	30.7	225	28.9
third abortion	11	8.0	5	5.7	67	8.6
fourth or more abortion	11	8.0	7	7.9	23	2.9
Total	137	100.0	88	100.0	779	100.0

Note: Non-respondents to questions on repeat abortions or ethnic group excluded. 'White' includes all non-black and non-Hispanic.

and despite her history there was still an air of optimism that this time things were going to work out and she would settle down and have the children she desired.

Previous surveys have suggested that there are a disproportionate number of abortions amongst non-white groups. We would expect this finding to be reflected in a higher number of repeat abortions. Table 5.23, however, shows only minor variations. It was the first abortion for 60 per cent of the white women and for 55 per cent of the black and Hispanic women. The percentages having their second and third abortions were broadly similar. The biggest difference was for those in for their fourth or more abortion. In the sample, the blacks and Hispanics were more than two and a half times as likely to have had multiple abortions as were white women.

Marital status and abortion   Some people seem to believe that if abortion was stopped altogether there would be a big increase in the population. In fact we know that there would be some rise but the vast majority of US women seeking abortions do intend to have children at a later stage. So for those interested in the likely effect of abortion on the population size, the marital status of the woman is obviously of crucial importance. Women tend to have abortions at two stages of their childbearing. The largest group are the single women who plan to have children at a later stage. The abortion rate amongst these women probably has little effect on the birthrate over the long period – the vast majority of them will carry on to have children at a time in their life when they are ready to bring them up. Married women are able to continue in an unplanned pregnancy without social disapproval, although they may have an abortion to space their children or because of financial constraints at the beginning of marriage. However, the crucial demographic effect on population in terms of abortion in the longer term is caused by those women who have abortions at the end of their childbearing period.

It has been argued in the past that married women seeking abortions have on the whole been less sexually active than single women. If that were the case then we would expect the age of first intercourse to be lower for the single. Table 5.24 reveals some evidence of single women beginning their intercourse at a younger age. Just over one in five had their first intercourse before the age of 16 compared to only one in six of the married women. They were also more likely to have had intercourse for the first time at the ages of 16 and 17 than the married women. However, these differences are not very large and it could be that the result is a reflection of the overall declining age at first intercourse. Furthermore, the sample of single women contained a proportion of early starters who at the time of the abortion were below the age of 16. Consequently the main conclusion is that there is little variation between the

Table 5.24 Age at first intercourse by marital status

Age	Single		Married		Widowed/ divorced/ separated	
	No.	%	No.	%	No.	%
15 or under	171	21.8	31	16.0	24	16.0
16–17	301	38.3	72	37.1	69	46.0
18–19	220	28.0	49	25.2	41	27.3
20–24	78	9.9	32	16.5	15	10.0
25–29	1	0.1	5	2.6	1	0.7
30–34	2	0.3	—	—	—	—
not known	12	1.6	5	2.6	—	—
Total	785	100.0	194	100.0	150	100.0

Note: 'Single' includes those of unknown marital status.

different groups according to marital status and the age at first intercourse.

We have seen several reasons to expect that those who are in a stable relationship are more likely to be regular users of birth control. This is likely to show up in married women being pregnant because of birth control failure rather than non-use. Table 5.25 shows that the married women were the least likely not to be using any method at all. However, the differences are not great and it might seem surprising that more than seven out of ten married women were not always using birth control at the time of conception. A high proportion of married women were using birth control only some of the time and, unlike the evidence for Britain, it was the widowed, divorced and separated women who were the most likely to reply that they were always using birth control.

One point I noted was that relatively few women discussed their impending abortion with their parents. A possible reason might be that once women have married and moved away from their family's home they are less likely to trouble it with their problems, especially where they have a partner who gives them support. I therefore tabulated the results according to marital status. Table 5.26 in fact shows very little difference according to marital status. In terms of telling their mother, the percentage is more or less the same for both single and married women. However, the percentage is slightly lower for those

Table 5.25 Birth control use at conception by marital status

Use	Single		Married		Widowed/ divorced/ separated	
	No.	%	No.	%	No.	%
thinking of using	96	13.8	17	10.5	11	9.6
sometimes using	221	31.8	55	33.7	33	28.4
always using	159	22.9	47	28.8	36	31.0
not using	219	31.5	44	27.0	36	31.0
Total	695	100.0	163	100.0	116	100.0

Note: Non-respondents excluded. 'Single' includes those of unknown marital status.

Table 5.26   Parental discussion of the pregnancy by marital status

Relationship	Single No.	%	Married No.	%	Widowed/ divorced/ separated No.	%
father	51	7.6	9	5.3	7	5.4
mother	133	19.8	32	19.4	22	17.1

Note: Based on a response rate of 671 single, 165 married and 129 widowed, divorced and separated women. 'Single' includes those of unknown marital status.

who are widowed, divorced or separated. There was a slight tendency for the fathers of single women to be more likely to know. However, only about one in thirteen did know about the pregnancy and in many cases this was presumably because the mother found out and told the father rather than because the daughter discussed the issue in terms of emotional support and decision making.

Catholics and abortion   The attitude of the Catholic Church to sexuality has led to great conflict for its members. The ban on artificial contraception has meant that the vast majority of members disobey the official teachings of the Church on this issue. Furthermore, when this ban is combined with the doctrine of chastity there is an additional set of problems for the single. The theory is that young people should wait to have sex until they are married and then should just use so-called 'natural' methods of birth control. This doctrine has meant that there is no official recognition of premarital sexuality and so no birth control education. To some people the recognition of sexuality would serve only to encourage 'promiscuity'. However, it has been argued by Fr. Andrew Greeley that the Church's attitude to sex in general and birth control in particular has led to a falling off in church attendance (Francome, 1984a). Individual Catholics I have interviewed have confirmed this view. A mother of two teenage children told me of her adolescent conflicts over her sexuality:

I couldn't decide whether or not to have sex. It was as if I had to choose between having a good time or remaining faithful to the Church. At the age of 17 I decided. I had sex and did not go near a church for a year. Then one day I was in New York City and went to a church on 33rd or 34th street. I decided to go to confession and tell the Priest I was having sex. I didn't want just to confess to the sex so I went in and told him that I had not said my night prayers and that I had had intercourse. He just told me to say Hail Mary's for the night prayers and didn't say anything at all about the sex. So I thought if that's the Church's attitude they can keep it.

She went on to say that she didn't return to the Church.

However, although there have undoubtedly been those who have been alienated from the Church by sexuality, others have just chosen to disagree with it on that issue. In fact, church attendance amongst Catholics in my sample was above that of the rest of the sample, as Table 5.27 shows. In order to take account of the facts that black attendance at church is higher than that of the rest of the population and that blacks were less often Catholics, I have separated the results by race. Out of the 133 blacks responding to the question there were twenty Catholics. Table 5.27 shows that white Catholics were twice as likely to have been in church in the previous month as non-Catholics. Nearly half the black Catholics in the sample had been to church in the previous week. When the results of the

Table 5.27 Catholic church attendance by race compared to rest of sample

Last attendance	White Catholic %	Other white %	Black Catholic %	Other black %
past week	19.4	10.2	45	18.6
past month	28.8	14.0	25	34.5
past year	22.5	24.6	5	15.0
not in past year	29.3	51.2	25	31.9
Total	100.0	100.0	100.0	100.0
Number	417	541	20	113

Note: Non-respondents to questions on religion or church attendance excluded. 'White' includes all non-blacks.

black and white Catholics are combined, over one in five (20.6 per cent) had been to church in the previous week and a further three in ten (28.6 per cent) had been in the previous month. So in all almost exactly half the sample had been to church in the previous month.

I also found in my earlier research into 1,000 students on Long Island that those who were more regular church attenders were more likely to oppose abortion than the rest of the sample. So it could be that there are a minority of Catholic teenagers who obey the laws on chastity and would not use abortion. However, one problem for the sexually active practising Catholic who does become pregnant is that the potential shame of a baby conceived outside wedlock is so difficult to face that abortion seems the best alternative. I received comments such as this from a man of 23, who opposed his girlfriend's abortion but felt he had to support her right to make the final decision:

> My girlfriend was brought up to wait until marriage but times change. She wants the abortion because she feels it's the right thing to do. She doesn't want a shotgun marriage. She wants me to marry her when I'm ready to do it and not be forced into it. Also she does not want to be found out. She comes from a religious family so there is fear there. I feel to hell with everybody, to hell with what people say. When the baby was born people would not reject it. People love kids.

As far as I know his girlfriend went ahead with the operation. This kind of example shows how in some ways those who have a 'respectable image' to keep up may in fact be more likely to have an abortion than those who are less concerned with appearances and more willing to run the gauntlet of public opinion.

I have stated that there are certain conflicts inherent in Church doctrine over sexuality. In some cases this might result in parents being unable to discuss sexual matters with their children. The results of my survey (see Table 5.28) show that in terms of giving information about menstruation there is a broad similarity between Catholics and non-Catholics. There is the same pattern of more than three young people in five being

Table 5.28 Catholic source of first information about menstruation compared to rest of sample

Source	Catholic		Non-Catholic	
	No.	%	No.	%
mother	269	62.4	369	63.2
father	2	0.5	2	0.3
friend	10	2.3	13	2.2
teacher	23	5.3	41	7.0
sibling	15	3.5	21	3.6
relative	8	1.9	4	0.7
doctor	0	0	5	0.9
no one	104	24.1	129	22.1
Total	431	100.0	584	100.0

Note: Non-respondents excluded. 'Non-Catholic' includes those of unknown religion.

told about their periods by their mother and over one in five not knowing what to expect.

The question about the discussion of birth control was answered by 417 Catholics. Just over one in fifty (2.4 per cent) said they had discussed it with their father and just under three in ten (29.3 per cent) had discussed it with their mother. These figures are significantly lower than those for non-Catholics. Although only 6.1 per cent of non-Catholic women had discussed birth control with their father, this is a much higher percentage than that for Catholics. More than two in five (41.4 per cent) of non-Catholics had discussed birth control with their mother. So it does seem that, while the Catholic Church's attitude to sexuality has not influenced patterns of discussion of the menstrual period, it has led to less discussion of birth control within the family environment. So it could be that Catholic young people's sexuality has to be more hidden from the family view.

In all 421 Catholics replied to the question about telling someone about their pregnancy. Just one in twenty (5.0 per cent) had told their father; one in six (16.4 per cent) had told their mother. Again, this is below the figures of 8.5 per cent and 21.7 per cent for non-Catholics, although in this case the differences are less marked.

Table 5.29   Catholic birth control use at first intercourse compared to rest of sample

Method	Catholic		Non-Catholic	
	No.	%	No.	%
pill	72	15.5	118	17.8
IUD	2	0.4		
diaphragm (cap)	15	3.2	28	4.2
sheath	86	18.5	119	17.9
withdrawal	76	.16.3	73	11.0
safe period	18	3.8	35	5.3
suppository	5	1.1	14	2.1
foam	18	3.8	34	5.1
not using/not known	174	37.4	242	36.6
Total	466	100.0	663	100.0

Note: 'Non-Catholic' includes those of unknown religion.

One point of interest is whether Catholics used the birth control methods favoured by their Church to a greater degree than the rest of the population. Table 5.29 shows very little influence of religion on birth control use at first intercourse, and such differences as do emerge are not as would be expected. Perhaps the most surprising fact is that more non-Catholics than Catholics said they were using the safe period. A slightly higher percentage of Catholics were not using any method at all. Male methods were more often used in Catholic women's first experience of intercourse: Catholics were 50 per cent more likely to use withdrawal and also a little more likely to use the sheath. Female methods were correspondingly less used by Catholics.

The results for birth control use at conception show a broad similarity (see Table 5.30). However, the two groups did show some differences. Catholic were less likely to be always using birth control and less likely to be using it sometimes, but also less likely not to be using it at all. Although the numbers were relatively small, they were 70 per cent more likely to answer that they were thinking of using it. This suggests that a few Catholics were having conflicts over use. A counsellor at a birth control centre in New York told me: 'Many Catholics believe that abortion is killing but they are not willing to take

Table 5.30   Catholic birth control use at conception compared to rest of sample

Use	Catholic No.	%	Non-Catholic No.	%
thinking of using	69	16.9	55	9.7
sometimes using	125	30.6	184	32.5
always using	93	22.8	149	26.3
not using	121	29.7	178	31.5
Total	408	100.0	566	100.0

Note: Non-respondents excluded. 'Non-Catholic' includes those of unknown religion.

the pill. If they took the pill every day they would be committing seven sins in a week. Abortion is a big sin but you get it out of the way.'

This argument is also put forward by Bill Baird (*Boston Globe*, 9 January 1981). However, I have not met any people seeking abortions who have used the argument, and I would suggest that people do not make a rational decision that, in terms of the number of sins, it is better to have an occasional abortion. Rather what happens is that they are in conflict over their sexuality in general and possibly see themselves as largely adhering to the Church's teaching. They obey the injunctions against premarital intercourse most of the time and only sin when intercourse occurs. Arranging to go for birth control would imply a recognition that they were going to disobey the Church's dictates on a regular basis rather than seeing themselves as overcome by passion on certain occasions. This feeling leads many to be casual in birth control use and then to have to face the consequences of an unwanted pregnancy.

Baptists and abortion   The Baptists were the second largest religious grouping represented in the sample, with 112 saying this was their religious preference. Racially the Baptists were equally divided between fifty-four whites and fifty-four blacks, with four being of other racial groups.

Baptists exhibit a high frequency of church attendance. Table 5.31 shows that a quarter of the Baptists attended church in the

Table 5.31   Denomination and church attendance

Last attendance	Catholic No.	Catholic %	Baptist No.	Baptist %	Rest of sample No.	Rest of sample %
past week	90	20.6	27	24.5	49	9.9
past month	125	28.6	32	29.1	83	16.7
past year	95	21.7	20	18.2	114	22.9
not in past year	127	29.1	31	28.2	251	50.5
Total	437	100.0	110	100.0	497	100.0

Note: Non-respondents excluded.

previous week compared to just over one in five of the Catholics and less than one in ten of the rest of the sample. A further three Baptists in ten were in church in the previous month.

Age at first intercourse was similar to the rest of the sample. Just over one in five (20.7 per cent) had their first intercourse before the age of 16 and two in five (39.6 per cent) started at the ages of 16 and 17. One in five (19.4 per cent) used the pill at first intercourse, and in all two in five (41.7 per cent) used female methods. One in four used male methods and a third did not use any method.

Only two of the Baptists said that they had discussed birth control with their father, whereas more than two in five (43 per cent) had discussed it with their mother. One in five hd also told their mother about their pregnancy (21.5 per cent). At the time of pregnancy, under one in five of the Baptists (17.2 per cent) had been using birth control all the time, which compares with 22.8 per cent of Catholics.

Jews and abortion   In my sample there were twenty-four Jewish women. Although it was a small group the findings were instructive.

Orthodox Jewish law tends to be relatively anti-abortion, but the other two groups of Jews – the Conservative and the Reform – take a liberal view and in both Britain and the United States Jews have been among the most important activists in favour of abortion rights (Francome, 1984a). In general, the

Jewish religion has a different approach to sexuality than the Catholic Church. A Conservative Jew who had been an abortion patient in New York explained to me her view of the difference: 'Judaism is very liberal. We consider sex to be a Mitzvah, a blessing. It's one of the natural God-created urges and functions to be accommodated. The sexual urge is to be satisfied.' With people having these kinds of belief it is clear that members of the faith are not likely to suffer the same kinds of guilt as Catholics. However, I should point out that even this woman, while espousing the ideal of openness and while she discussed sexuality in general terms with her parents, nevertheless did not ever discuss with them the specifics of her own behaviour.

The sample did not attend religious services very often: only one of the twenty-four had been to a service in the previous two weeks. A further nine had been in the previous year but the other fourteen had not been in the past year. However, many Jews practise their religion at home. For example, the woman I quoted above told me that, although she only attended services on holidays such as Yom Kippur, the family always lit the Sabbath candles and observed dietary laws. At a Seida they would go through the order of service, although she commented that people would go through it fast to get to the food. In many ways she did not seem particularly religious, but she said that she was proud of Judaism, and would never date a non-Jew.

Every one of the Jewish women knew what to expect when their periods arrived: twenty-one were told by their mother, one by the school, one by the girl scouts and one didn't say.

The age at first intercourse was comparable with the rest of the sample. More than half of the twenty-four began their intercourse at the ages of 16 and 17. Three had their first intercourse at the age of 15 and the rest started over the age of 18. At first intercourse, nine used male methods (eight the condom and one withdrawal), nine used female methods and six did not use anything. Twenty-one responded to the question about use of birth control at time of conception: five were always using a method, seven were using a method some of the time and nine were not using a method. My interviews had led me to expect that Jewish women were much more inclined to use the diaphragm than other religious groups. There was some evidence of this in my sample. None reported being on the pill and four out of the five failures were from the diaphragm. Others reported that they had not used the diaphragm on that occasion. For example, one criticised herself: 'Sloppy, didn't want to stop and put diaphragm in.'

In all, the sample showed differences in some areas such as early sex information, lack of attendance at religious services and possibly patterns of birth control use. However, the group showed similarities in patterns of sexual behaviour and level of birth control use.

Ethnic groups in the USA   The different ethnic groups in the United States have wide variations in their family patterns. The Hispanic groups in the United States are in large part immigrants from Puerto Rico and are mostly Catholics, although without high religious observance. The variations are particularly noticeable between the blacks and whites, although there is some evidence of a narrowing of differences. For example, in 1982 three black mothers out of five (59 per cent) reported having their first birth before marriage compared to only one in ten (11 per cent) of white mothers (Pratt *et al.*, 1984, p.4). The national data also seem to indicate that blacks tend to start their sexual activity at an earlier age. In 1982, the proportions of never-married women aged 15–19 who had sexual intercourse was 40 per cent amongst whites and 58 per cent amongst blacks, although this difference was slightly less than that found in earlier surveys.

A narrowing of the differences was found in terms of the number of children born. In 1982, ever-married black women had on average had 2.5 children compared to 1.8 for white women. This was a drop in numbers for both groups since 1973 and the absolute difference narrowed, although the relative difference remained constant (Pratt *et al.*, 1984, p.10). The proportions of wanted births increased for both groups: they rose from 67 to 77 per cent for black women and from 88 to 91 per cent for white women. This suggests a great improvement in terms of children being brought into caring homes, especially amongst black women. However, by 1982 nearly a quarter of black births were still unwanted and this accounts for much of the fertility difference between the groups.

The age structure of my sample reveals that 26.5 per cent of whites were under the age of 20 compared to 23.7 per cent of blacks. Blacks were over-represented in the older age groups. This might seem a surprising finding, but it reflects the fact that those young blacks who do become pregnant are more likely to continue with the pregnancy. Within white culture this would be more open to censure and so an abortion might appear a more attractive alternative.

The history of a young man of 19 illustrates why blacks may be over-represented in young births but not abortions. He has a son of 2½ and his partner was only 14 at the time of the pregnancy. He told me:

> My son was not planned. It just happened that she got pregnant. I guess she used that as a way of trapping me and I had to marry her. She didn't want an abortion. When we got married she had sex with someone else. The guy told my sister and I found out about it. I left her. I told her, 'I can't trust you and so I can't base my relationship with you.' When I left her I was only 17 . . . I see my son every weekend. I'm seeing him today as a matter of fact. I buy all his clothes . . . I'm now living with someone else and she is on the pill.

The marital status of the different ethnic groups is shown in Table 5.32. This indicates that the percentage of married black women in the sample was higher than that for whites and Hispanics. This difference again suggests that single black women are much more likely to continue with the pregnancy and that abortion is more likely to result after childbearing than is the case with white and Hispanic women.

The question about knowledge of the menstrual cycle also reveals differences between the groups. Table 5.33 shows that three blacks in ten did not know what to expect when they began their periods. This is considerably higher than the figures of one in five for the white women. No blacks at all were first given the information by their father.

We have seen that national data suggest that blacks begin their intercourse at an earlier age than whites. This was not,

Table 5.32   Marital status and ethnic group

Status	No.	%	No.	%	No.	%
married	30	21.6	15	16.0	121	15.0
single	90	64.7	62	66.0	576	71.4
widowed/divorced/ separated	19	13.6	17	18.1	110	13.6
Total	139	100.0	94	100.0	807	100.0

Note: Non-respondents to questions on ethnic group excluded. 'White' includes all non-black and non-Hispanic. 'Single' includes those of unknown marital status.

Table 5.33   Source of first information about menstruation by ethnic group

	Black		Hispanic		White	
Source	No.	%	No.	%	No.	%
mother	67	58.2	48	57.1	496	65.7
father			1	1.2	3	0.4
other person	14	12.2	16	19.0	100	13.3
no one	34	29.6	19	22.6	155	20.5
Total	115	100.0	84	100.0	754	100.0

Note: Non-respondents to questions on menstruation or ethnic group excluded. 'White' includes all non-black and non-Hispanic.

Table 5.34   Age at first intercourse by ethnic group

	Black		Hispanic		White	
Age	No.	%	No.	%	No.	%
15 or under	25	17.6	19	19.9	177	22.0
16–17	60	41.8	31	32.7	327	40.7
18–19	41	28.7	32	33.7	217	27.0
20–24	16	11.2	13	13.7	80	9.9
25–29	1	0.7			3	0.4
Total	143	100.0	95	100.0	804	100.0

Note: Non-respondents to questions on age at first intercourse or ethnic group excluded. 'White' includes all non-black and non-Hispanic.

however, a finding of this study (see Table 5.34). In fact, it was whites who started earlier. The reasons for this difference are not clear. One possibility is that Louisiana, from where the majority of the blacks in the sample came, generally has a higher average age at first intercourse than the other states in the sample.

This result on average age at first intercourse is similar to the British data, which also found whites to have started earlier. However, the British finding that blacks were more likely to have their first intercourse with a casual partner was not found in the United States. In all the groups, the first intercourse was as part of a regular relationship in more than four cases out of five.

Previous observers have usually found some class differences between ethnic groups. This survey was no exception. Table 5.35 shows that only one in twenty of black fathers were members of the upper middle class compared to nearly one in five of the white fathers. White mothers were twice as likely to have upper middle class jobs than were the mothers of black women. Two in five of the parents of the black women were not recorded because they were absent, unemployed or retired. This contrasts with a figure of below three in ten for white women. So there are clearly status differences, which presumably have influences on behaviour.

Table 5.35   Social class and ethnic group

Social class	Black Mother %	Father %	Hispanic Mother %	Father %	White Mother %	Father %
upper middle	7.7	5.4	7.9	7.1	13.4	18.4
lower middle	36.9	21.7	23.6	20.0	39.2	26.2
upper working	7.7	19.4	12.4	21.2	10.1	17.2
lower working	8.5	14.0	20.2	22.4	10.1	9.7
none/unknown	39.2	39.5	36.0	29.3	27.2	28.5
Total	100.0	100.0	100.0	100.0	100.0	100.0
Number	130	129	89	85	783	786

Note: Non-respondents to questions on ethnic group or class excluded. 'White' includes all non-black and non-Hispanic.

Table 5.36 Church attendance by ethnic group

Last attendance	Black %	Hispanic %	White %
past week	22.8	16.0	14.7
past month	33.0	27.2	20.1
past year	13.5	23.5	23.6
not in past year	30.7	33.3	41.6
Total	100.0	100.0	100.0
Number	133	81	780

Note: Non-respondents to questions on church attendance or ethnic group excluded. 'White' includes all non-black and non-Hispanic.

We have seen in the section on Catholics that the blacks had higher church attendance. The full results for the ethnic groups are given in Table 5.36. This reveals clear differences. Of the three groups, the blacks were the most regular attenders, with over one in five attending in the previous week and a further third attending in the previous month. One in five of the white women had attended a service in the previous month and three in twenty went in the previous week. Attendance of the Hispanics was in between that of the other two groups.

Table 5.37 Birth control use at conception

Use	Black No.	%	Hispanic No.	%	White No.	%
thinking of using	11	9.1	22	25.9	82	11.5
sometimes using	46	38.1	21	24.7	234	32.7
always using	20	16.5	14	16.5	195	27.3
not using	44	36.3	28	32.9	204	28.5
Total	121	100.0	85	100.0	715	100.0

Note: Non-respondents to questions on birth control use or ethnic group excluded. 'White' includes all non-black and non-Hispanic.

We saw that fewer black women were given 'information' about the menstrual cycle. Table 5.37 gives comparable information about birth control use at conception. It reveals a clear difference between the whites and the other two ethnic groups in terms of always using birth control. Nearly three in ten of the white women said they were always using birth control compared to one in six of the other two groups. This evidence, together with that on menstruation, suggests there is a strong need to improve birth control education within minority groups.

Men, birth control and abortion

One fact that became abundantly evident from my research was that the double standard was still in operation. When during the 1960s there was talk of the 'permissive society' it was generally put forward from a theoretical perspective that the liberalisation of sexuality should apply to both sexes. However, what seems to have happened is that, rather than societies moving towards one standard of behaviour for all, there was a general loosening of the sexual restrictions but the overall double standard remained. So the male still tends to play the more assertive role while the female is more passive. I found the male often felt that his reputation was enhanced by his sexual behaviour while a woman was expected to be much more discreet. There are clear sex roles in the United States and this could be a factor in unwanted pregnancies. None the less, in the course of my research into the attitudes of men to abortion it became clear that underneath the general 'macho' image of the US male there was often a great deal of sensitivity.

The information about men in this section is derived from three main sources. One source was participant observation during my frequent visits since my first year as an exchange teacher. Second, I carried out thirty interviews with men accompanying their partners who were having abortions. These interviews were conducted on several occasions between 1978 and 1985. Third, information was gained from the data of 363 questionnaires collected in 1978 in Boston and New York (Francome and Francome, 1979). I did not collect questionnaires from the men at the time of the 1982–4 study because it would not have been possible to make the cross-cultural comparisons that are central to it. However, as data on men are relatively rare, they are clearly relevant.

Some people assume that men tend to distance themselves from an abortion. However, in the survey 52 per cent of white males attended the centres with their partners. As a quarter did not know of the abortion, over two-thirds of those who knew accompanied their partner. In other cases the woman and her partner decided together that it was better that he should work rather than take time off and lose pay at a time when their finances might be stretched by the cost of the abortion. Black men were only half as likely to accompany their partners as were white men.

First intercourse

As discussed in the Introduction, in other surveys of sexual behaviour the males *claim* to start an an earlier age than the females (Kinsey *et al.*, 1953; Schofield, 1965; Farrell, 1978). My respondents were no exception, as Table 5.38 shows. There is a broad similarity between the age at first intercourse for women in 1978 and in 1982–4: the first sample began its intercourse at a slightly younger age, but this can largely be explained by the fact that the first study was carried out only on the East coast while the second was based on a more representative sample. There is, however, a large difference in the replies from the men: nearly one male in five said his first intercourse occurred below the age of 14, compared to less than one in twenty-five of the females. Fourteen of the males claimed to have had their first experience of intercourse between the ages of 5 and 9; in five of these cases their partners were reported to be a similar age. So it seems that there is a minority that is sexually active before puberty, a practice that has been common in certain primitive cultures (Malinowski, 1929) and also sometimes happens in Britain. One question of interest is why pre-pubertal sex was not reported by the female sample. It could be that it is much less common because a few young girls service a larger number of boys. However, it may also be the case that, as young boys get kudos from their sexuality, they are more likely to report it. Women may often feel that early sexual experiences as children are not particularly relevant.

In general terms it seems that men are much more likely to have their first sex with a casual partner and for the incident to have little long-term significance other than that the boy concerned has had some sexual experience. I interviewed one 19 year old in February 1985 and he told me of his early sexual history:

> I had my first sex at the age of 13. The girl was 14. It was very casual. My friend just asked me if I wanted to have sex and he called the girl up on the phone. She came round with two friends. My friend had sex with one of the other girls and things were relatively easy because his mother was at work . . . . When I was 16 we used to try and compete with our friends. We'd go out and see if we could pick a girl up and see if you could do this or see if you could do that. Then we would go back and say how we had got on . . . . My mother found out I was having sex when I was 18. I had a letter in my trouser pocket from this girl I had been having sex with and my mother found it when she went to do the washing. The letter said that she was looking forward to having sex with me again and one or two other things. My mother didn't say anything she just came in and threw the letter on the bed. I thought 'I don't care' and that she should mind her own business. I don't think my father would mind.

This kind of attitude is reflected in the answers the sample of men gave to the question about their relationship to the person

Table 5.38 Age at first intercourse

Age	Female sample (1982–4) %	Female sample (1978) No.	%	Male sample (1978) No.	%
13 or below	3.4	28	3.8	60	18.8
14–15	16.9	145	19.6	65	20.3
16–17	39.8	318	43.1	122	38.1
18–19	27.9	175	23.7	57	17.8
20 +	12.0	72	9.8	16	5.0
Total	100.0	738	100.0	320	100.0

Sources: Francome and Francome (1979) and this survey. Non-respondents distributed in proportion.

Table 5.39   Relationship with partner at first intercourse

Relationship	Female sample (1982–4) %	Female sample (1978) No.	Female sample (1978) %	Male sample (1978) No.	Male sample (1978) %
husband/ steady	82.0	662	87.8	173	53.2
casual partner	16.1	75	9.9	99	30.5
pick up	n.a.	9	1.2	37	11.4
other	1.9	8	1.1	16	4.9
Total	100.0	754	100.0	325	100.0

Note: Non-respondents distributed in proportion.

at the time of first intercourse. Table 5.39 shows that men were ten times as likely to have their first intercourse with a 'pick up' and more than three times as likely to have had it with a 'casual partner'. They were much less likely than women to have had their first sexual experience with a person with whom they were in a steady relationship.

Even so, it is important to point out that more than half the male sample had their first intercourse as part of a steady relationship. A 23 year old I interviewed in 1985 explained to me that he had had sex only with his current girlfriend who was in for an abortion. He contrasted his attitude to that of some others:

> These guys all say 'I do it with anyone I can get my hands on.' I never looked at it this way. I always felt something. It's hard for me to break up with girls. I never had sex when I was young but when you know the opportunity's there it's not so bad.

So, although the double standard of sexual behaviour is very strong, it would be a mistake to view all young males as avidly pursuing sex. In fact, in my interviews with women I have come across numerous cases of those who would have had sex much earlier but their partner did not feel their relationship was sufficiently developed.

Birth control use

The birth control methods for men are much less problematical in that there is no waiting time, no large fee to be paid and no need for physical examinations. Furthermore, as the males are socialised to be sexually active, they have less conflict in terms of losing their 'pure' self-image. The sample of males was asked how often they used condoms. One in twenty-five (3.7 per cent) said they always used them, just over half (56.3 per cent) said they sometimes used them and two in five said that they never used them (40.0 per cent). So, in all, three in five males had some experience of the use of the condom. However, it seems that many men would only use birth control under pressure from the woman and that in many cases they did not feel much responsibility for their own actions in possibly causing an unwanted pregnancy. Those who did use condoms often reported that it was under some kind of duress, as the following comments from a 23-year-old ex-marine and a 21-year-old clerk showed. I asked them if, when they were going out for the evening, they would plan to use birth control. Their replies were:

> If the girl was less easy going I guess the guy would go out and buy something. But if the girl isn't going to insist on it I guess the guy isn't going to bother. It's her responsibility. Probably 80 per cent of guys think it's the girls responsibility. Most of us don't go asking her 'Are you on the pill or whatever?' We carry on and, if she lets you, go ahead. It is permissive of the girl. If I go out with a girl for a while then I ask her. If it's just like a pick up one night you don't bother about it. That's 60 per cent of the problem. The girls don't care or don't think about it.

> I'd carry on and I'd only use it if she wanted me to. If that's the only way you are going to have sex then you'd put it on. But if you can get away with it you're not. But it's like there if you need to have it . . . . It should definitely be up to the girl. Any guy can potentially get any girl pregnant. It's up to her. Either it's cool, she knows she is going to get her period tomorrow or it's not and she knows that.

These kinds of comment reveal a strong divide between the sexes and some antagonism.

However, on rare occasions I found some concern, as with a 22 year old who worked in a garage:

> At the last minute I say 'Are you protected?' That's me you know. Some guys don't give a shit and if they don't say nothing and don't do nothing they'll just assume, you know . . . . I give my word.' If they are not protected I say 'Do you want to keep going?' Hey, she's got to know what she's doing. It's pretty well up to the girl to say 'Hey, I'm not protected be careful'. If she says 'be careful' I pull out at the end.

The males were also asked what they liked and disliked about the condom. Table 5.40 reveals strong feelings against the condoms. Two-thirds of those responding said there was nothing they liked about them. Those who did have some

Table 5.40 Men's attitudes towards condoms (1978)

	No. of men	%
Favourable aspects:		
none	125	67.2
birth control, safety	31	16.6
easy to obtain	11	5.9
protect against VD	5	2.7
prolong sex	4	2.2
male can use	3	1.6
no side-effects, cheap, portable	7	3.8
Total	186	100.0
Dislikes:		
insensitivity	70	35.3
everything	48	24.2
interrupts sexual act	13	6.6
break, come off, fail	18	9.1
not natural	13	6.6
tight	9	4.5
inconvenient, awkward	6	3.0
embarrassed to buy	3	1.5
other	18	9.1
Total	198	100.0

positive feelings stressed birth control use, easy accessibility and protection against venereal disease. Those disliking them stressed insensitivity and inconvenience. The phrase 'It's like having a shower with your raincoat on', kept reoccurring. One in ten mentioned contraceptive failure as a problem. One 21-year-old young man told me with more than a hint of irony:

> Whenever it was a bad time I'd pull out. I didn't bother a week before and a week after her period. It is ironic. I screwed around for two years then the first time I used the bags, that month, she got pregnant . . . . I didn't put them on at the beginning. I would hang out for a while and then put them on at the end. You see I live at home and she lives at home but we've had the house for a month so we've been doing it a lot more and we just put them on for protection.

Some boys told me they were too embarrassed to buy contraception. One 16 year old obtained his condoms by stealing them from his father's drawer. However, once he had stopped doing this for fear of being discovered, he did not get any alternative supplies. Increased availability of slot machines could well help with this problem.

Men's attitude to the abortion

The men I interviewed were, as one might expect, usually in favour of their partner having the abortion. Sometimes, as with the second of the comments below, there is a show of bravado:

> It's the least of all evils. She works and I don't want to marry her. I have to get my bachelor's and then master's and so I have four or five years. If she's still around then I will marry her . . . I don't think being here is the greatest thing but its the only way out. [20-year-old student]

> It's got to be done. She knows that and I know that. We don't like being here . . . . I hope she is O.K. by this afternoon so we can go to the Coliseum for the car show. [21-year-old mechanic]

On the other hand, others showed concern about the situation. John was 23. His father had recently died, just before the parents' twenty-fifth wedding anniversary, and he felt sorry for his mother and that he also had to care for his two sisters who were 14 and 18. He did not like the thought of the abortion at all.

> I tell you the truth it's her choice. I really don't like it. It hurts a lot. She is my first girlfriend. I keep thinking it could be my girl or boy. I don't want to argue with her. I would have preferred her not to get pregnant . . . prefer to stay single. I will stay with her. I will marry her but it must come at the right time. Sure we will get married. That's why I don't want the abortion done. May never have another chance like that. What if it was your only chance? . . . . Both of us are at fault. It's just for love. She's not mad with me, I'm not mad with her. You try to make the other one happy. We're both sensitive. I don't want a shotgun wedding but I think in time people wouldn't worry about it. The last couple of nights I haven't slept. Last night I know she didn't. All I keep thinking is 'Is it a little girl or boy?', but it's her body and we're not married.

In all, the general impression I received from my numerous interviews was that there was a strong degree of concern. The young men were very cavalier about birth control use but they realised that abortion was a more serious issue. Of course, those who did not attend with their partner would be likely to contain a higher proportion of those who were not concerned.

Conclusion

This chapter indicates that the abortion rate in the USA varies a great deal between states, but that overall thirty women in 1,000 women of childbearing age have an abortion each year. It also shows that most abortions are carried out before 9 weeks' gestation.

Other major findings were the lack of communication in terms of sexuality between parents and children and the strong differences between the sexes. Although two-thirds of mothers were the source of their daughter's first information about menstruation only just over a third of them had discussed birth control with their daughters and less than one in five had discussed the pregnancy. There is even less communication between fathers and daughters on the question of sex. In less than half of 1 per cent of the cases was the father the first source of his daughter's information about menstruation, and less than one in twenty had discussed birth control with their daughters. So it comes as a little bit of a surprise that as many as one in fifteen knew of their daughter's pregnancy. This lack of communication across the generations is a crucial problem in terms of teenage sexuality.

I discovered a strong tendency for men to regard birth control as the woman's responsibility. Men seemed to take the view that they could go around having intercourse as often as possible but that it was up to the woman to ensure that she did not get caught with an unwanted pregnancy. Until men are socialised to take more responsibility for their sexuality and to have more consideration for women, there are clearly going to be a great deal of unwanted pregnancies. This is something that will be discussed further.

In general terms, I found a lack of birth control use. This might be more understandable for those who were very young having sex for the first time. However, this lack of use seems to continue for many. In the sample there were 110 women who were having a third or subsequent abortion and only a quarter of these were always using birth control. So there is a case for people to be socialised into taking a more responsible attitude towards sex, for parents and children to begin discussing it, for men to use birth control or to ensure that their partner does so, even in a casual relationship, and for women not to take so many chances.

It is clear from comparative evidence that the abortion rate in the United States could be greatly reduced by a more rational and open approach towards sexuality. The comparative data in the next chapter will suggest some of the changes that can be made, and these will be discussed more specifically in the Conclusion.

6 Comparison between Britain and the United States

This chapter first considers the differences in the number of abortions between Britain and the United States together with wider comparisons. It then analyses related factors before attempting to explain the reasons for the differences between the countries.

The number of abortions in Britain and the USA

Table 6.1 shows that the abortion rate in the United States was more than twice that of England and Wales. We have seen further that the Scottish abortion rate for 1981 (including those

Table 6.1 Abortion numbers and rates: England & Wales and the USA, 1973–84

Year	England & Wales All	Rate per 1,000 women, 15–44	United States All	Rate per 1,000 women, 15–44
1973	110,600	11.5	744,600	16.3
1974	109,400	11.5	898,600	19.3
1975	106,200	11.0	1,034,200	21.7
1976	101,000	10.4	1,179,300	24.2
1977	102,700	10.4	1,316,700	26.5
1978	111,900	11.3	1,409,600	27.7
1979	120,600	12.0	1,497,700	28.8
1980	128,900	12.8	1,553,900	29.3
1981	128,600	12.5	1,577,340	29.3
1982	128,500	12.3	1,573,900	28.8
1983	127,400	11.9	1,515,000	27.4
1984	136,400	12.6	1,508,000	26.9

Sources: OPCS, Ref AB 84/6; OPCS (1984); OPCS (1985); Tietze (1983) p.33; Henshaw *et al.* (1985).

travelling to England for their operations) was only 9.2, which is a third that for the United States.

These data can be put in even wider context by including information from a number of selected countries. Table 6.2 shows that the highest rate in Western Europe is in Italy. However, even here the rate is well below that in the United States, which has the highest abortion rate amongst developed Western societies. The rate for the Netherlands is only about a fifth of the rate in the United States and half that of England and Wales, despite the fact that abortion is easily available. This low rate is due to a number of factors. The general efficiency of the Dutch obviously stands them in good stead in terms of birth control use, and they also have a high proportion of sterilisations.

Eastern European countries tend to have higher abortion rates than Western ones although there are wide variations. The Soviet Union is considered to have the highest abortion rate in the world. However, exact data on this are not forthcoming. Fuller discussion of abortion in different countries is contained elsewhere (Francome, 1984a).

Here, I am more concerned to compare data for Britain and the United States and further light on the differences between the two countries can be shed by comparing abortion rates according to various characteristics.

Characteristics of abortion population

Age

Table 6.3 shows that, although the abortion rate in the United States is higher than that in Britain at all ages, there is nevertheless wide variation in the level of the discrepancy. It is at the lower age ranges that the United States has the highest comparative rates. For those under the age of 15, the United States had more than four times the rate of abortions than did Britain. In the age groups 15–19 and 20–24 the United States' rate was about two and a half times that of the British. However, amongst women over the age of 30 the difference narrows. The United States rate for those aged 30–34 is less

Table 6.2 Legal abortion rates of selected countries

Country	Year	Rate per 1,000 women, 15–44
Western Europe:		
Italy	1980	22.4
Netherlands	1983	5.9
Scotland	1982	7.6
France	1979	14.1
German Federal Republic	1982	6.8
England and Wales	1984	12.6
Sweden	1984	17.7
Norway	1984	15.9
Denmark	1982	19.3
Finland	1984	12.3
Iceland	1983	12.8
Eastern Europe:		
Poland	1978	18.3
Czechoslovakia	1984	34.4
Hungary	1983	35.5
German Democratic Republic	1977	22.5
Yugoslavia	1975	58.5
Soviet Union	1970	180.0[a]
Bulgaria	1978	68.3
Canada	1980	11.5
USA	1984	26.9
Hong Kong	1980	8.6
Singapore	1983	27.9
India	1984	3.3[b]
Japan	1980	22.5[c]
Tunisia	1979	14.6
Cuba	1980	47.1
New Zealand	1983	9.8
Australia	1975	21.7

Sources: Tietze (1983); Henshaw (1985); Chen, Emmanuel, Ling and Kwa (1985); and primary sources.

Notes:

a This estimate is very tentative and awaits more information.

b There are many illegal abortions not counted.

c Data known to be incomplete.

Table 6.3   Legal abortion by age: England & Wales and the USA, 1981

| Age | England & Wales | | United States | | |
	Number ('000s)	Rate per 1,000 women, 14–44	Number ('000s)		Rate per 1,000 women, 14–44
under 15	0.8	2.0	15.2		8.6
15–19	34.1	19.3	433.4	15–17	30.1
				17–19	61.8
20–24	34.3	18.5	554.9		51.1
25–29	21.9	13.2	316.3		31.4
30–34	18.7	9.7	167.2		17.7
35–39	12.7	7.6	69.5		9.5
40 +	5.4	3.1	20.8		3.4
not known	0.6				
Total	128.5		1,577.3		

Sources: *Abortion Statistics* (1981) p. 3; Henshaw *et al.* (1985); and primary sources (OPCS personal communication).

Note: The rate for the under-15 age group is based on the population of women aged 14 and for the 40+ age group on the population of women aged 40–44.

than double the British rate and over the age of 35 there is relatively little difference between the two countries.

So clearly it is in the younger peak age groups that the major explanations for the differences in overall abortion rates need to be sought. These differences will be discussed later.

Abortion gestation

A minor reason for the higher number of abortions in the United States might be the difficulty of access. There is some evidence that British abortions take longer to procure. Using the latest data available, Table 6.4 shows that more than half the abortions in the United States occur under 9 weeks gestation compared to just over a third in Britain. Furthermore it shows that 60 per cent more abortions in Britain occur after 13 weeks. Part of the explanation of this could be that in Britain a higher percentage of abortions are for foetal abnormality, and occur later. However, this can account for only a small fraction. The private sector abortions occur earlier than the NHS ones. However, even here the British time span is greater than that in the United States. This is further

Table 6.4 Length of gestation at abortion: England & Wales and the USA

| | England & Wales | | | United States |
| | | (1983) | | (1981) |
Weeks of gestation	All %	NHS %	Non-NHS %	All %
under 9 weeks	34.5	22.7	45.9	51.4
9–12	50.9	64.5	38.0	39.8
13–20	13.6	12.4	14.8	7.9
21 +	0.9	0.4	1.3	0.9
not known	0.1	0.1	0.0	
Total	100.0	100.0	100.0	100.0

Sources: OPCS (1985); Henshaw *et al.* (1985).

evidence of the delays within the British system discussed in Chapter 4 and confirms the need for the British system of care to be improved so that women are not made to wait unnecessarily for their treatment.

Number of children

I mentioned in my earlier discussions that in Britain in particular abortions occurred at two major stages of women's lives. They were likely to take place either during the teens and early twenties, before the woman had developed her living conditions to a degree where she felt she could have children, or at a later stage in life when she had completed her childbearing. It is therefore instructive to make some comparisons of abortions by the number of children.

Table 6.5 shows that in both countries just over half the women presenting for abortion had already had one or more children. The data do, however, reveal a number of differences between the two countries. The major one is that in Britain women were more likely to have had two previous children than one. They were also more likely to have had more than three children than one child. This fits in very well with the point about the second main area of demand for abortion coming

Table 6.5   Abortions by number of children: England & Wales and the USA, 1981

No. of children	England & Wales No. of abortions	%	United States No. of abortions	%
none	67,400	54.1	911,880	57.8
one	16,746	13.4	312,200	19.8
two	23,498	18.9	219,880	13.9
three	11,050	8.9	84,480	5.4
four or more	5,861	4.7	48,900	3.1
Total	124,555	100.0	1,577,340	100.0

Sources: Henshaw *et al*. (1985); OPCS (1983).
Note: The US data are for living children and the British for living and still born. Total number of abortions for England and Wales excludes 4,026 cases where the number of children is unknown.

from women who had finished their child bearing. Those women who only want one child or became pregnant soon after a birth and use abortion for spacing are relatively few in number. However, in the United States this pattern was not borne out. Among US abortion patients, a higher number of women had had one child than had had two children and more than twice as many women had had one child than had had more than three children. A possible explanation for this is the higher rate of sterilisation and hysterectomies amongst US women. Some research has suggested that in the United States there are more than twice as many hysterectomies per head of the population compared to Britain (Bunker, 1970). We also know that the rates of sterilisation are much greater, although exact comparative data are not available. These factors are clearly important in influencing the abortion rate for women after childbearing has been completed; if it were not the case, the overall difference in the abortion rate between Britain and the United States would be even greater.

Marital status

Both the official and the sample data on marital status (see Table 6.6) show that in Britain a higher percentage of women

Table 6.6   Marital status: Britain and the USA

Status	Britain (1983) Survey sample %	Official %	United States (1981) Survey sample %	National %
married	25.4	30.2	17.2	18.9
single	61.5	57.5	67.9	
widowed/ divorced/ separated	11.3	11.0	13.3	81.1
not known	1.8	1.3	1.6	
Total	100.0	100.0	100.0	100.0

Sources: OPCS (1985); Henshaw *et al.* (1985); and this survey.

were married compared to the United States. In terms of abortion, this clearly ties in with what I have said about the fact that married women who had completed their childbearing were more likely to use sterilisation in the United States. It also begs further questions about behaviour amongst the American singles that leads to their abortion rate being so high and this is discussed later in the chapter.

Repeat abortions

The higher abortion rate in the United States would lead one to expect a higher percentage of repeat abortions in my sample. Table 6.7 shows that more than two in five of the US sample were receiving their second or subsequent abortion compared to less than one in five in Britain. In comparative terms the greatest different was, however, amongst women who were receiving their third abortion or more: less than 3 per cent of British women fell into this category compared to more than 12 per cent of US women. So the higher percentage of multiple abortions is clearly a factor in the different abortion rates between the countries.

Teenage pregnancy

We have already seen that the differences in the abortion rates

Table 6.7 Previous abortions for the total sample:
Britain and the USA

Previous abortions	Britain	United States
none	81.9	58.9
one	15.4	28.8
two	2.2	8.1
three	0.2	2.8
four	0.3	1.4
Total	100.0	100.0

Note: Non-respondents distributed in proportion.

between Britain and the USA were greatest amongst the
teenagers. In 1985 a useful study was published by the Alan
Guttmacher Institute and reported in the *New York Times*
(*NYT*) on 13 March 1985. This compared teenage pregnancy
rates in thirty-seven developed countries and provided more
detailed examination of six countries selected because they were
felt to resemble the United States closely in terms of
socioeconomic and cultural characteristics and because they had
accumulated data on teenage sexual activity. The countries
chosen were Britain, Sweden, France, the Netherlands and
Canada. The information for the project was collected from
questionnaires sent to foreign embassies in the United States,
from American embassies abroad and from the family planning
agencies in the countries studied. Further data were obtained
from published reports and visits of about a week to each of the
countries used as a case study.

The evidence showed that the United States had both a
higher number of teenage births and a higher number of
teenage abortions than the other countries studied. In terms of
births the report stated:

> Teen-age birthrates are much higher than those of each of the
> five countries at every age (15 through 19) by a considerable
> margin. The contrast is particularly striking for the younger
> teen-agers. In fact, the maximum relative difference in the
> birthrate between the United States and other countries
> occurs at ages under 15. With more than five births per 1,000

girls aged 14, the United States rate is around four times that of Canada, the only other country with as much as one birth per 1,000 girls of comparable age [*NYT*, 13 March 1985]

In terms of abortion the United States also had a higher rate. By the time they were 18, sixty out of every 1,000 women in the United States would have had an abortion. This was twice the level for the next highest countries (France and Sweden) where the comparable figure was about thirty. In Canada, it was twenty-four and in Britain just over twenty. By far the lowest rate was in the Netherlands, where the figure was only seven per 1,000 – less than an eighth of the US level.

In seeking the reasons for the differences, the report discounted three commonly held views. First, it argued that the explanation could not be due to differences in the level of sexual activity, because these were roughly the same in the countries concerned. Nor could the availability in the United States of maternity and welfare benefits be seen to be a factor. In fact, the report noted that in most countries the overall level of support seemed to be more generous than in the United States. Thirdly, it said that, although the birth and abortion rates of non-white groups were higher, they could not account for the differences.

The report argued that a crucial factor was the lack of use of contraceptives in the United States, especially of the pill with its lower failure rates. Countries with greater availability of birth control and sex education had lower teenage pregnancy rates. It also noted a difference in attitudes between governments as to their role in preventing unwanted pregnancies. It suggested that most countries set out to prevent pregnancy without making a judgement on the morality involved. This contrasted with the United States where the dominant view had been that the government should try and prevent teenage pregnancy by preventing sexual activity and promoting chastity. At a news conference, the Dutch sociologist Evert Ketting commented: 'In Holland, we felt it was time to get rid of old taboos. We never discuss the question of "Should teenagers have sex?" Teen-agers can and do talk out their ambivalences and their feelings, and we think of it all as human relations' (*NYT*, 13 March 1985).

In my sample in the United States there were thirty-two patients presenting for abortion at the age of 16 or under: one 13 year old, four 14 year olds, eight 15 year olds and nineteen 16 year olds. Those aged 15 and under had not used birth control methods either at first intercourse or at the time of conception, although in rare cases their partner had used condoms. There was some sign that the anti birth control legislation was a factor. For example, a 14 year old from Boston had written about her lack of birth control use: 'Did not ask permission from parents.' The 16 year olds showed more sign of birth control use: at time of first intercourse five were using the condom, two withdrawal and one the safe period; three were on the pill. Among all those aged 16 and under, six out of the twenty-eight respondents were always using birth control at the time of conception. This was a slightly higher proportion than that for the British sample, where only one in six of those 16 and under always used birth control. This kind of evidence suggests there is a great need to target the young groups and stress that if they are going to be sexually active then they should be so in a responsible manner.

Possible reasons for the differences in abortion rates

There are a number of factors that could potentially lead to the United States having a higher abortion rate. First of all the fact that abortion is more easily accessible in the United States could result in a greater number of abortions for a variety of reasons – couples could be more likely to take risks as they knew the constitution protected the right to an early abortion, for example. However, abortion is available in Britain from a number of sources, albeit with some delay, so I do not think availability is a very important factor. Secondly, American teenagers may be at risk for a longer period because sexual behaviour occurs at an earlier age and is more likely to be unprotected. Thirdly birth control services are more widely available in Britain, especially to young teenagers, and they are free. Fourthly, cultural factors may affect both the relationship between parents and children and that between the sexes.

Finally, there may be a lack of alternatives. I shall consider these factors in more detail.

Age at first intercourse

We saw that the Alan Guttmacher Institute report suggested little difference in the age at first intercourse between Britain and the United States. However, there had not been a British teenage sex survey for ten years prior to the publication of their report. The evidence from my sample indicates that women in the United States began their sexual activity earlier than those in Britain (see Table 6.8). Just over one in ten of the British sample had intercourse at the age of 15 or below compared with one in five of the United States sample. However, the British sample was more likely to have their first intercourse at the age of 16 or 17 so in both countries by the age of 18 about six women in ten had had intercourse. The survey did not ask anything about the frequency of intercourse or number of partners, which are clearly relevant factors. Evidence presented later will suggest that both are likely to be greater in the United States.

Birth control use

The questions about birth control revealed significant differences between the two countries. The first is that, while just

Table 6.8   Age at first intercourse: Britain and the USA

Age	Britain No.	Britain %	United States No.	United States %
15 or under	74	11.8	226	20.3
16–17	269	43.0	442	39.8
18–19	186	29.7	310	27.9
20–24	85	13.6	125	11.2
25–29	7	1.1	7	0.6
30–34	3	0.5	2	0.2
35–39	2	0.3		
Total	626	100.0	1,112	100.0

Note: Non-respondents excluded.

over a quarter of the British respondents said they were not using any method of birth control at first intercourse, in the United States the proportion was well over a third (see Table 6.9). A major reason for this difference is the variation in men's usage of birth control. For three British women out of ten a condom was used at first intercourse contrasted to less than one in five in the United States. Withdrawal was also less likely to be used in the States, and although it is less reliable it is better than nothing. The methods of birth control more likely to be used in the States included the diaphragm, suppositories and foam. The last two show the influence of commercial factors. These methods are relatively unreliable and are not recommended in the British family planning services. In the United States, however, they are sold over the counter.

A second significant difference is that two out of five British women were always using birth control at the time of conception compared to less than one in four American women.

Comparing birth control use according to marital status reveals that less than a quarter of single women in the United States were always using birth control at the time of conception, compared to well over a third in Britain (see Table 6.10). This finding could be accounted for by the several differences I noticed between the cultures in my interviews and

Table 6.9 Birth control use at first intercourse: Britain and the USA

Method	Britain		United States	
	No.	%	No.	%
pill	135	20.8	190	16.8
IUD	3	0.5	2	0.2
cap (diaphragm)	12	1.8	43	3.8
sheath	195	30.0	205	18.2
withdrawal	104	16.0	149	13.2
safe period	26	4.0	53	4.7
suppository	3	0.5	19	1.7
foam	4	0.6	52	4.6
not using/not known	167	25.8	416	36.8
Total	649	100.0	1,129	100.0

Table 6.10   Birth control use at conception by single women: Britain and the USA

Use	Scotland No.	%	England & Wales No.	%	United States No.	%
thinking of using	5	12	40	10	107	13.2
sometimes using	8	19	105	26	254	31.3
always using	16	37	142	35	195	24.0
not using	14	32	118	29	255	31.5
Total	43	100	405	100	811	100.0

Note: Non-respondents excluded. 'Single' includes the widowed, divorced and separated, and those of unknown marital status.

participant observation. For example, there seems to be a more rational attitude towards sex in Britain and birth control is discussed more openly. Research carried out by the Health Education Council in 1977–9 showed an overwhelming majority of young men in Britain felt contraception to be a joint responsibility – 77 per cent amongst the 16–18 age group rising to 84 per cent among the 22–24 year olds (Family Planning Association, 1984). Unfortunately there are no comparative data from the United States on this question.

In my private interviews I found that some British men felt that their peers did not care too much about birth control: 'I don't think that guys as a rule bother too much about birth control. They just take it for granted that the girl is sensible. They ask about it afterwards. They're too much in love with their tool' (24-year-old former student). Others have even admitted that they themselves do not often concern themselves too much: 'I usually don't bring it up. I don't go out of my way to mention it. I know it's a real chauvinistic attitude but there you are' (clerical worker).

On the whole, however, the British men are more likely to see themselves as having some responsibility for ensuring that they do not cause an unwanted pregnancy.

When I meet a woman and we are getting on well and it seems that we might sleep together I always broach the subject of birth control. I always keep a few condoms in the car in case of emergency and so I never have to take risks. [21-year-old student]

I don't normally say anything until things have gone pretty far. In that way I know it will be O.K. Then I say 'Are you on the pill or anything?' If she says 'No', I go and get my Durex. [23-year-old entertainer]

These comments reflect the fact that the British (both male and female) are considerably less prejudiced against condoms than the Americans – although there are the usual criticisms:

I find them a bit awkward. They interfere. In the middle you have to sit back and put them on. You don't get the same sensitivity . . . I think my attitude to them can be summed up by the joke: 'What's the similarity between a hat from a Christmas cracker and a condom? . . . In both cases you feel like a fool putting it on but it helps to make the occasion'.

Others have condoms available on the less laudable grounds that they may be needed at the insistence of the woman: 'I might carry condoms if I thought the opportunity might be imminent. So then they can't use that excuse. I say I've got them in the cupboard' (19-year-old student).

Indeed, it seems that British women are more likely to insist on birth control being used. Some men have told me of occasions when they have missed out on having sex because they did not have condoms with them at the time. For example, a journalist commented: 'I went out with her and we were getting on really well. We went to bed and were laying there with no clothes on. But she wouldn't let me fuck her because I didn't have any johnnies. We never did get to do it.'

This same respondent told me of another incident when he was sent out to get protection by a Scottish woman:

I was talking to the Scottish Jane in the pub one lunchtime and we began discussing things. I began asking her about sex and she asked me about birth control. I said I didn't have anything with me so she said it would be O.K. if I bought some. I thought she was having me on but she said she wasn't so I rushed out and got some and we went back to her place.

This kind of rational discussion about birth control right at the start of a relationship does not seem to occur that much in the United States, and possibly occurs more in Scotland than in England and Wales – although the results for the single Scots women were similar to the English, I very often came across the assertion that the Scots were much more rational and practical about birth control.

I have not said anything so far about withdrawal as a method of birth control; in fact, some US counsellors will not count it as a method at all. We have seen that the withdrawal method is over-represented in the failure rates and should not be used on a regular basis. However, it is better than nothing and can be used quite successfully for short periods. Indeed, amongst certain unskilled groups in England I have observed that it is recommended and that the information is passed on. A 19-year-old builder's labourer told me: 'My brickie told me about sex. He said what you do is leave it in for a while and then when you get a funny feeling you pull it out quick. I always do that. I always say that you'll never get a woman into trouble unless you do it drunk and forget to come out. I never do it when I'm drunk.' A few years ago I had a debate with a 24-year-old student about condoms. He said he did not like to buy them as it meant he would have less to spend on drink and statistically withdrawal was just as good. I didn't convince him and not long afterwards his girlfriend became pregnant and they got married. He argued that it was just one of those things and you can't say much about a random sample of one.

Table 6.11 shows that birth control usage amongst married women also varies greatly according to country. There were only nine Scottish women, but all of them said they were always using a method of birth control at the time of conception. Despite the smallness of the sample, this result was highly statistically significant. Just over half the sample for England and Wales and less than three in ten of the American sample were always using birth control. So the lack of use of birth control in the United States seems to continue into marriage.

Those women who did not use birth control were asked the reason. Table 6.12 reveals a broad similarity in the responses between Britain and the United States. In both countries the

Table 6.11 Birth control use at conception for married women

Use	Scotland No.	Scotland %	England & Wales No.	England & Wales %	United States No.	United States %
thinking of using	0	0	9	7	17	10.5
sometimes using	0	0	33	26	55	33.7
always using	9	100	63	49	47	28.8
not using	0	0	24	18	44	27.0
Total	9	100	129	100	163	100.0

Note: Non-respondents to questions on marital status or birth control use excluded.

Table 6.12 Reasons for not using birth control: Britain and the USA

Reason	Britain %	United States %
thought sterile	5.8	7.1
had intercourse unexpectedly	40.4	48.3
cost	0.8	4.4
did not know of any	0.8	1.2
did not know where to go	3.3	3.9
intended to use but had not made an appointment	17.0	23.4
religion says it is wrong	2.7	2.0
stopped using because of side-effects	29.7	26.7
hoped pregnancy would lead to marriage	2.2	0.2
did not intend to have intercourse anymore	8.2	6.8

Note: Percentages based on the number of respondents who did not always use birth control. In Britain this was 364 and in the USA 659.

primary reason for not using birth control was that they had had intercourse unexpectedly: nearly a third in the United States gave this as their reason. A further 5 per cent in each country said that they did not intend to have intercourse any more, so presumably their sex act was unexpected. The second most important reason in both countries was that they had

stopped using birth control because of its side-effects – one in
five gave this as their reason. It was largely users of the pill
who were having problems and they did not change to an
alternative method. The minor reasons did show some
differences. Women in the United States were five times as
likely to mention cost. However, the fact that any woman in
Britain mentioned cost at all is surprising since birth control is
free. Several British women mentioned the fact that they hoped
their pregnancy would lead to marriage. This did not occur in
the United States to such a degree. Surprisingly there was no
difference between the countries in the number who said that
birth control was opposed by their religion.

The overall conclusion from this table is that women in both
countries face similar kinds of problems in terms of the
inadequacies of available birth control methods and the kind of
birth control to use when an unplanned opportunity for
intercourse occurs. This section has made it clear, however,
that British men and women do seem to be more assiduous in
the use of contraception and this is clearly a factor in the
differences in the abortion rates between the countries.

Parents' attitudes to sex and birth control

In both Britain and the United States we have seen that there is
a lack of communication between the generations in terms of
sexuality. Very often parents do their very best to ignore their
children's sexual activity, and if they know that it is occurring
expect their children to be discreet and keep it from view.
Conversely, many teenagers are shocked to find evidence of
their parents' sexuality. Some of these problems were investigated by Ginoff (1969). He reported comments by parents in
the United States such as:

I find it terribly upsetting when my daughter asks me
questions about sex.

Whenever my teenager asks me about sex, my face turns
crimson, I freeze, I stutter.

I once said that two rabbits got married. I couldn't bring
myself to use the words mate or copulate in front of him.

In my research, I have found similar examples of parents not being able to communicate with their children. As far as many parents are concerned, their children do not have any sex until they get married. Even then, some parents react as if their grandchildren were born by immaculate conception.

The data I collected about discussion of birth control provide comparative evidence (see Table 6.13). In both societies 36 per cent had discussed birth control with their mothers. However, there seem to be few like the Catholic mother I reported (p.120) who accepted her daughter's sexuality and supported her in her use of birth control. In both societies father's and brothers' involvement was much less than that of mothers and sisters. So the statistical analysis shows little difference between the countries concerned. The only differences of note were that American women were more likely to have discussed birth control with their girlfriends or sisters.

Similar comparative data about discussion of pregnancy are tabulated in Table 6.14. Here, there are clear differences between the countries. Nearly three in ten British patients for abortion had discussed their pregnancy with their mother, compared to less than one in five of the women in the United States. This difference is also seen in terms of discussion with fathers: although less than one in five British women discussed

Table 6.13   People with whom the sample had discussed birth control: Britain and the USA

Relationship	Britain No.	%	United States No.	%
no one	32	5.3	45	4.5
father	38	6.3	45	4.5
mother	220	36.2	361	36.3
brother	28	4.6	51	5.1
sister	153	25.2	327	32.8
girlfriend	267	43.9	585	58.8
teacher	24	3.9	39	3.9
partner	456	75.0	727	73.1
other	79	13.0	85	8.6

Note: Percentages based on response rates of 608 for Britain and 994 for USA.

Table 6.14 People with whom the sample had discussed the pregnancy

Relationship	Britain No.	Britain %	United States No.	United States %
father	108	17.7	67	6.7
mother	180	29.5	187	18.7
no one	23	3.8	70	7.0
brother	53	8.7	57	5.7
sister	123	20.2	180	18.0
girlfriend	238	39.1	477	47.7
partner	474	77.8	726	72.6
other	74	12.2	81	8.1

Note: Percentages based on response rates of 609 for Britain and 965 for USA.

their pregnancy with their father, this was still nearly three times the level of discussion amongst American daughters and fathers. If we consider just women who were not married, for whom discussion with parents is probably more relevant, the difference between the countries is even greater. Nearly a third of the single British women had discussed their pregnancy with their mother and one in five had discussed it with their father. In contrast less than one in five single American women had discussed their abortion with their mother and only one in thirteen with their father. These figures suggest that the lack of discussion across the generations is far more marked in the United States, alhtough some would argue that the communication gap is much too great in both societies. The fact that parents and children even when living in the same house do not know about such significant events in each other's lives obviously raises a great many questions about sex taboos in the so-called permissive society.

Cultural factors and the abortion rate

So far I have discussed the access to abortion, age at first intercourse, birth control use and parental relationship in terms of the comparative abortion rates. However, the wide variations cannot be explained by these factors alone. It seems that cultural factors, especially amongst the young, are crucial in understanding the different levels. It is to these influences that I now turn.

A good place to start the discussion is a small pamphlet written by Margaret Mead during the Second World War called *The American Troops and the British Community* (1944). It aimed to reduce some of the tensions between the US army and the indigenous population. The pamphlet pointed out that many of the conflicts were due to the fact that Americans were often stationed in large numbers near towns and villages too small to accommodate the extra men looking for a good time. However, there were also many conflicts of norms. The British, for example, placed great store on people standing upright and regarded it as a sign of spinelessness and indiscipline to slouch. Mead suggested that the Americans, in contrast, saw 'no harm in taking the weight off their feet by leaning against the nearest wall in sight'. She drew attention to some of the reasons for other cultural differences – for example, the fact that America was a relatively new country and so could not value things that were old and instead concentrated on the new.

Mead also pointed to the fact that a high proportion of United States society was made up of immigrants who were relatively unsure of themselves: 'In no other country in the world have there been so many parents who were not cocksure of how to live in the world, so many parents who expected their children, even as quite small children, to speak better English, to know their way about in the world better than their parents did' (p.7). As a result, many of the problems that were arising were within the context of relationships. Mead drew attention to the fact that in the United States there had always been a shortage of women, so American men were much more assertive than the British. She argued, too, that the American males enjoyed the company of women more than the British.

One major difference to which Mead drew attention was the dating system, which did not have a British equivalent. She argued that members of neither sex wanted a date with an unpopular partner and that once on a date each needed to justify their popularity:

the boy by boldly demanding innumerable favours, the girl by refusing them. If the boy should fail to bid for a hundred kisses this would prove that he had a low opinion of himself, but if the girl gives in she thereby proves that she has a low opinion of herself, that she isn't sure that if he had not booked the evening, someone else would have done so. A really successful 'date' is one in which the boy asks for everything and gets nothing but a lot of words; skilful, gay, witty words' [p.11]

She went on to say that these kinds of norms were very confusing to British girls. Some were annoyed at the speed of approach of the US male, while others took his advances as if they 'came from a British boy' and possibly thought the serviceman was proposing when he wasn't and wanted to take him home to meet her father. So Mead points out that in many cases there were conflicts of norms. However, we may also note that in many cases the Americans were indeed proposing, and consequently there were many GI brides.

The differences in the youth cultures between the societies in terms of their dating patterns have continued. Waller had outlined the essential features of the situation in the United States as early as 1937 and other researchers had continued to explain the development. They reported a very formalised system, with the young men asking the women for dates well ahead of time. By Wednesday the girl should have fixed up her date for the Saturday night. Anyone ringing late for a date would be considered to have insulted her. Sexually, the double standard was very strong. As Mead intimated, the man was meant to make advances and the woman to refuse them.

This rigid dating system seems to have broken down during the 1960s. In fact, by 1977 when teaching in New York, older people in my classes surprised the younger ones when talking of the rigidity of the dating system of their youth. With the liberalisation of the 1960s it became more acceptable to have premarital sexual relationships and the emphasis on dating could easily lead to a high number of sexual partners. This is especially true for those who became sexually active while still relatively young and possibly dating a wide variety of partners.

However, although there were not the same kinds of restraint in terms of rigid ringing up for dates, some traditional features still remain. The fraternities and sororities are still around, although with nothing like their earlier prestige. There is still a great deal of competition within the youth culture, which is fostered by the schools. There are still well-produced 'year books' from high schools with pictures of the Homecoming King and Queen, references to the person most likely to succeed and to the most popular person. There is also still a great deal of prestige attached to sport.

The old double standard, too, has been maintained. This was shown clearly in a survey I carried out in 1978. The study was based on 797 single students aged 17–20 on Long Island, New York, and was reported under the headline 'Briton's study finds double standard on sex' (*Newsday*, 13 July 1978). This showed widely differing attitudes to casual sex. One of the questions asked students whether they agreed with the following statement: 'Boys should not go to bed with someone they have just met, for example, at a party.' Only one in five of the boys agreed with this compared to three in five of the girls. The males were also more likely to support females having casual sex. Only three in ten of them said that girls should not go to bed with someone they had just met at a party, compared to seven out of ten of the females. So the sexual divide was quite clear. However, it was not the traditional double standard where men wanted to be sexually active themselves and marry someone relatively innocent. Both males and females showed a large degree of internal consistency, but the males were clearly socialised to pursue a much more liberal attitude towards sexuality than the females. Roberts' (1985) work points in the same direction. He has suggested that, while there is a loosening of the norms, the basic patterns of the relationship have continued:

> All the relevant British and American inquiries have found that young people worry about personal relationships, particularly their ability to 'sell' themselves to the opposite sex . . . . It becomes part of the currency in sexual negotiations. Girls sell favours and boys pay out, the terms of trade being set by the partners' relative ratings. Youth cultures mediate wider social mores, and teach females to use

their sexuality to build social relationships, while males learn to use sex for personal gratification, and pay with status earned in the wider society. [p.80]

I would suggest that, although double standards operate in both societies, nevertheless various structural and historical factors make the differences in standards far less marked amongst the British. This is particularly the case with students. For example, the British grant system means that for the three years they are at university both male and female students have a similar amount of money and so the traditional patterns of relationship with the male paying for dates and providing the transport cannot be maintained.

In addition, the British youth culture differs a great deal from the American pattern. Amongst the majority non-student population a crucial feature is the male peer group. This is a group, usually of four–six members but possibly numbering over twenty, that forms the basis of the adolescent's social life. One of the best early discussions of British youth culture was that of Allcorn (1955). He found that peer groups grew from children's play groups and reached the peak of their activity at the age of 16–18 when all the young men in his area of study preferred spending time with a peer group. They went out together at least five nights a week, with Saturday night being almost sacred. There was no belief in sex equality in the groups and it was felt that the best time was to be had when all the males were together. The groups were against the development of relationships with women except for sex. Allcorn commented: 'When one of them was going out with a girl, the others subjected them to a continuous stream of satirical and bawdy comments.' A boy could most easily justify going out with a girlfriend rather than the group by making allusions to real or imagined sexual activity. This comment is similar to those reported on pp.8–9.

My research into British youth culture found that it had not changed very much in its essential features (Francome, 1976a). I contrasted the culture of the women with that of the men. The culture of the teenage females was very pro-marriage while that of the male was against marriage. This main feature of the culture has remained until the present time. There is little evidence of female peer groups; females are much more likely to join together in pairs. The boys join peer groups about the age of 13 or 14 and these form the basis of their social life. In many ways the culture is very supportive of the young men. The fact that the peer groups are against members spending too much time with girls means those who have little success with members of the opposite sex can find comfort in being loyal peer group members. It is therefore possible to be a social success without dating on a regular basis or having a regular girlfriend. In fact, the groups are rather censorious of those who are too involved in relationships. This is a crucial difference from the situation in the United States and is linked to the lack of competitiveness in the British culture over a wide range of activities. The peer groups stress equality and are supportive of their members. A second important difference is that of the role of the dance. In the US couples tend to date and go to dances together. In Britain, in contrast, the boys tend to go to dances with their peer groups and the girls with their best friend or a small group. My evidence on where young people met their partners found the dance to be by far the most important place for developing new relationships.

When I did my original research, a respondent described a popular London discotheque as follows (Francome, 1976a, p.132):

> Every week it's the same. It starts at 7.30 p.m. and until 9.00 only the girls dance. They do a kind of skinhead step that they have obviously been practising. They all get in a line and kick their legs together. The boys stand around drinking until about 9.00 p.m. then they start moving in. After 11.30 p.m. the youngsters (15 and 16 year olds) leave to catch their buses home. The older ones stay on till 12.00 p.m.

These days there are more examples of males dancing together, but the essential features are the same. The format is such that it is very difficult to fail: the music is loud so there is no need to make polite conversation, the couples do not touch in the early part of the evening and it is dark so any teenage blemishes are not so visible. The boys leave their peer groups in couples and dance with pairs of girls for one or two records before moving on. If couples are interested they may go for a drink with each other. Later in the evening the dancing becomes slower and more intimate and sometimes a request may meet refusal. Some teenagers develop significant signals with their friends to express interest, while others use more informal methods:

> When Jill and I are dancing a slow dance, we get close to the boys and have our hands on their shoulders, we watch each other's eyes. Otherwise when the dance is ended, if I don't fancy him I just say 'Thank you' and turn away, then she turns away too unless she really likes her boy. This does not happen very often, however, because there is a code between us that we must stick together because if one of us goes off with a bloke, the other is left on her own.

Couples who meet at dances will often arrange to go out somewhere in the following week. Older teenagers sometimes have informal arrangements to meet at the dance and go home together afterwards. However, once a relationship develops, the dance diminishes in importance. The growth of relationships also conflicts with the peer groups, which become decreasingly important and usually break up entirely on marriage, although the Allenbrooke group, which I studied for a number of years, still meets each Sunday lunchtime at their traditional pub.

Attitudes to sex are generally positive amongst the peer groups, which often help their sexually inactive members to get some experience. The Allenbrooke group used to have girls who attached themselves and who dated various boys in the group. One went out with four different members before marrying the fifth. One of the Allenbrooke boys did not believe in sex before marriage at first because of religious reasons. The group, however, encouraged him to change his mind and he became by far the most promiscuous in the group.

> We put him in a position where he could not back out and from then on he never looked back. A year ago he came to us and said three more for my hundred. At first we thought 'no' but then we began to count up and we realised it was right . . . If a frog hopped by he'd screw it.

However, this kind of behaviour was unusual and at times he

missed important group activities because he was seeking romantic liaisons. The others preferred to spend all their time with the group, and did not often seem willing to devote time developing relationships. In Swindon they found it easy to get girlfriends but when they were off their home patch it was much more difficult. A good example occurred when eight of the Allenbrooke group went on holiday to Spain. They produced a 'European Expedition Report', which contained details of scoring methods. For sex the points were as follows: 'Fellatio 150, Intercourse 100, F.A.M.O. [female assisted manual orgasm] 50, Fondling Female Genitals 25, Masturbation minus 10.' They clearly left with great ideas of wild sexual adventures. However, after the holiday the report showed that none of them had been with any women at all. What was more interesting was that, despite the bravado, only the 'randy' one bothered about it. He complained to me that the others were only interested in drinking and they wouldn't go with him to search for girlfriends so he found it difficult to operate.

In fact the British peer groups seem to go through two stages as regards casual sex. When the participants are relatively young (up until the age of 16), they actively pursue sexual experience, anytime and more or less with anyone. Yet when they become a little older they become more discriminatory and there is prejudice against spending time seeking sex for its own sake. Typical comments were: 'When I was young I was always out for a screw but now I'm older I'd rather have a wank than spend time with someone just for one thing' (18 year old). So there are ambivalent feelings about casual sex and the groups do tend to frown upon it, especially in so far as it interferes with peer group activity.

I would suggest therefore that there are significant differences between British and United States youth cultures in relation to sex and that these are very important in understanding the differences in abortion rates. There is much less need in Britain to prove oneself in terms of the ability to succeed in relationships and there is not the pressure on the sexes to begin dating at an early age, although the strong sex divide leads to a lack of communication in many cases. Moreover, it seems to be the case that in the United States young men are encouraged to be much more assertive about their sexuality.

Table 6.15   Rates of rape in Britain and the United States (per 100,000 population)

Year	Britain	United States
1973	2.0	24.5
1975	2.1	26.3
1977	2.1	29.1
1978	2.5	30.8
1979	2.4	34.5
1980	2.5	36.4
1981	2.2	35.6
1982	2.7	33.6

Sources: USA – US Department of Commerce (1983) p.176);
Britain – Home Office (1984) p.38, and *Annual Abstract of Statistics.*

One piece of evidence that supports this is the different rates of rape in the two societies (see Table 6.15). We know that the official figures are a gross under-estimate and most researchers suggest there are at least five times as many rapes committed as are reported. It has also been suggested that part of the measured increase in rape might be due to women becoming readier to report it because of the help they now get from the women's movement (Wilson, 1983, p.62). The setting-up of the London Rape Crisis Centre in March 1976, for example, clearly gave women added support. However, from a comparative viewpoint there is no reason to assume that US rapes are reported to a greater degree than the British. Table 6.15 shows that for the last year for which there are comparable data the rate of rape in the United States was twelve times that for Britain. This is a remarkable difference and, in my view, may well be an under-estimate, because Britons are probably less suspicious of the police than are Americans.

In explaining differences between rates of rape in different societies Toner (1982) has used anthropological evidence as a starting point. She noted that in Kenya the Gusii had very hostile and aggressive relationships between clans and that this persisted in the relationship between the sexes:

The wedding night sexual performance is of immense importance to the status of both husband and wife. The husband is determined to force his wife into a position of subordination by repeated acts of intercourse, preferably to hurt her so much that she is unable to walk the next day. The bride is determined to resist to the utmost, to bring shame on her husband. The act of intercourse is seen as an act of subjugation of the female and as such it continues to be important [Toner, 1982, p.52]

She went on to report that the Gusii had very high rates of rape, which in 1955–6 were 47.2 per 100,000 population. She contrasted them with the Arapesh, whose views of sex were very much opposed to compulsion. The evidence she produced suggested that amongst this group rape was not known and in fact the kind of male nature that would commit such an act was unknown to them.

Toner suggested that in Britain the attitude towards sexuality was nearer that of the Gusii than the Arapesh, that the social structure is characterised by ignorance and antagonism and that children are raised to accept powerful distinctions in the expected behaviour of the sexes. She further suggested that in all Western cultures it is socially acceptable to take women by force: 'Men should desire and conquer; women must be desirable and conquerable. Yet while men should be masterful and assertive, women should be chaste and innocent' (1982, p.55).

One can agree with Toner in seeing that the sex roles of men and women lead to problems. In as much as men are required by the society to be sexually assertive and take the lead in initiating relationships while women are expected to be relatively 'pure', then there are clearly going to be wide differences in perspective. We can see that rape is just the polar end of the 'normal' patterns of relationship. The question is how far this explanation helps us to understand the differences in the rate of rape between Britain and the United States. This could be a book in itself so I will confine myself to some preliminary observations. I suggest that, although Toner is right to point out that in all Western societies there is a double standard, nevertheless there are significant differences between Britain and the United States. The level of violence is much greater in US society and the murder rate is about ten times that of comparable European countries (Lea and Young, 1985). There is also a much greater tendency for men to be assertive and for them to be unconcerned with women's feelings. I have given some data on this from Margaret Mead's earlier work, but in general it is difficult to illustrate by more than anecdotal evidence. However, the use by men of the phrase 'barefoot and pregnant', which suggests the role of sex and pregnancy in ensuring that a woman is kept within her traditional role, is one that does not occur in Britain. It is only a phrase but I suggest that it is illustrative of a difference in attitude between the cultures. There is also a great deal of hostility from women towards men in the United States. One story that was retold by a group of feminists in 1979 was of a biologist who was raped by four men. She did not get angry but said to them would they like to go back with her for coffee. Once back she slipped drugs into their drinks and while they were asleep castrated them all. This story seems a little unlikely. However, the point is that it was retold and her actions greeted with such phrases as 'Right on'.

These important cultural differences also influence sex even when it is performed by consent. As we have seen in various interviews, the US male has been prepared to make statements along the lines that 'women should look after themselves'. Any movement to reduce the abortion rate must therefore involve fundamental changes in the relationship between the sexes. This is of course going to be a problem within the American context because there is a staunch body of opinion that believes firmly in segregated sex roles. For example, in an interview in 1977, Spencer W. Kimbell, President of the Mormon Church stated:

> Man and woman are two different kinds of being. He's hard and tough. He's supposed to furnish the family's livelihood. She's more tender and unless a husband dies or the children are grown, we feel she ought to remain at home and teach children the things they should know. Therefore, we feel differently from many people towards the woman's movement and programmes that take women away from the home [*US News and World Report*, 19 December 1977]

Such comments are not by any means exceptional. Writers

such as George Gilder (1981) have been applauded for making similar statements and his books widely distributed amongst the White House Staff.

Alternatives to abortion

A final factor in the difference in the abortion rates is that in the United States it is less socially acceptable to have a baby outside marriage. Especially outside the minority groups, much greater stigma is attached to illegitimacy and women are more likely to be encouraged to give up the baby for adoption than in Britain. There is also the problem of cost. In the United States, for a woman not on Medicaid the cost of the birth is likely to be about $2,000–3,000, so once a woman is pregnant the cost of the abortion is relatively small. For many women in Britain becoming unexpectedly pregnant there is free delivery, a small maternity grant and social services to help them keep their baby. They may possibly be supported in the decision by the family. The response to an unwanted pregnancy in Britain is therefore less likely to be abortion.

Conclusion

There are clearly a number of factors involved in the difference in the abortion rate between Britain and the United States. The combination of even less sexual education, greater taboos on discussion of sexual matters within the family, wider segregation of sex roles, and lack of support for having a baby outside marriage means that the US abortion rate is much higher than that in countries that are comparable in some other respects. In some ways, the situation in the United States might be seen to be analogous with that in Britain at the start of the 1970s. At that time, both teenage births and abortions were at a high level, presumably caused by an increase in sexual activity unaccompanied by improvements in birth control use. However, as was reported earlier, by 1980 the number of births to teenagers had dropped dramatically: for every five in 1970 there were only three in 1980 when population size is taken into account. Less than a seventh of this reduction was due to an increase in the number of abortions, which suggests that birth control education can reduce unwanted pregnancies. Dutch evidence indicates that by identifying the necessary changes and putting them into operation it is possible to reduce the number of unwanted pregnancies even further.

7 Conclusion

In my comparisons of the social life of Britain and the United States I have identified a number of problems in terms of the relationship between the sexes. I have shown wide differences between the abortion rates of the two societies, and in passing I have mentioned even lower rates in countries such as Holland. These data suggest that both the British and the United States abortion rates could be much lower if changes were instituted. In the United States it would seem reasonable to aim to reduce the number of abortions by half over a five-year period, while in Britain a 25 per cent reduction would seem reasonable over a similar period. This would be achieved by improving services along the lines suggested below.

Improvements in sex education

There was a time when sex outside marriage was regarded as a sin, with a baby outside marriage or venereal disease as the 'punishment'. When a cure for venereal disease was discovered just before the First World War there were those who bewailed the removal of an important prop to civilisation, which would lead to promiscuity. Sex education is opposed on the same grounds. However, in modern-day societies, where sexual stimulation is a regular part of the mass media and often used as part of a sales technique for products with nothing directly to do with sex, it could hardly be expected that teenagers could not think about sex, even if this were felt to be desirable. So, rather than schools just ignoring the problem, they have a responsibility to deal with it in an appropriate manner.

We have seen great gaps in both Britain and the United States in even the most elementary sex education. The fact that a quarter of women in both societies did not know what to expect when their periods arrived; the fact that a woman did not know that the first experience of sexual intercourse is sometimes painful and that men ejaculate; the fact that many men and women do not come to terms with their own sexuality so that each experience of intercourse comes as a surprise – these are the kinds of problem that could be dealt with quite successfully by developing suitable sex education programmes. In addition, the British evidence indicates that sex education can be effective in reducing unwanted pregnancies. Catholic schools will of course wish to stress the value of chastity, but there are natural aspects of sexuality that cannot be avoided even among those who plan to be celibate. I have stressed menstruation as an area of lack of knowledge for young women, but young men may often experience a great deal of worry if, for example, they wake in the middle of the night, find they have ejaculated and yet do not know why.

Those who object to sex education on the grounds that talking about the subject will make matters worse are in a minority, even in the United States. Thus, in 1982 Gallup found that 70 per cent of Americans were in favour of sex education in public schools (Shostak and McLouth, 1984, p. 222). This percentage should rise now that more evidence is being provided of the need and if the fears could be allayed by open discussion and by making teaching materials available to parents and politicians. Clearly, care must be taken to ensure that courses are appropriate for the age of the child. However, many useful programmes are already in operation and in many respects the problem is largely a technical one of implementation.

We know that the vast majority of people will have sex before they are married, and they have to make decisions about the conditions under which this should happen. One would hope that both those who decide to have premarital sex and those who choose to wait until marriage will find it a good experience and one on which they will look back with some affection. One would also hope that care will be taken to ensure that an unwanted pregnancy does not result.

In 1955, when the Swedes introduced sex education in schools they made it part of the curriculum to tell pupils that sex before marriage was wrong (Linner, 1968). This is something that they do not do these days. The problem about an overall belief in chastity is that it does not distinguish between a wide variety of different relationships. The condemnation of all pre-marital sex precludes any discussion about the quality of relationships and what safeguards are taken against pregnancy. In this sense it is counterproductive.

Improvements in birth control services

The British birth control services are far in advance of the American ones in terms of the degree of support from the government. Free birth control was introduced in Britain in 1974 and on the whole it has been a great success. The Brook Advisory Centres have been particularly successful in catering for the needs of young people.

Although there have been great improvements in the British system of health care, I have nevertheless identified various areas where there is need for improvement – the main one being the fact that men have been discouraged from attending birth control clinics. We have seen that in the early acts of intercourse men have been involved to a greater degree than women in birth control. But their attendance at birth control clinics is so low that when a survey of the 1,880 family planning clinics in England and Wales was carried out in 1981 the results could not be used 'because we had overestimated the lowest number of men attending clinics. We had expected the number of males attending clinics to be low, but were not prepared, as the wording of our question shows, for such a low attendance' (Chambers, 1984). One of the seemingly strange findings of a survey published in 1982 was that only 7 per cent of condoms were provided free through family planning clinics. Local doctors do not 'prescribe' them and, although a few were provided free through the family planning domiciliary services, the rest were purchased largely at chemists. Of the condoms distributed through family planning clinics, less than 1 per cent were given to men and more than 99 per cent to women (Chambers, 1984).

The evidence from my survey makes it clear that men's lack of attendance at birth control centres is not due simply to the fact that they do not wish to take responsibility in this area. The fact is that they have been discouraged from attending. Chambers suggested the reasons as follows:

> Either because they consider that family planning clinics are only for women, or are unaware that free supplies of condoms can be obtained. Even where they do know this they are usually too embarrassed to use the service because of the predominance of women attending and staffing the clinics. [Chambers, 1984, p. 4]

However, she also commented that most of the clinics would welcome men and wished more would attend. So there is a case to be made for setting up a different environment in the family planning clinics. In particular, I would like to see special nights when men's health is discussed with lectures and films, and when there are discussions of the role of men in relationships.

I also feel that the United States should begin to consider seriously what to do about the health of its teenagers. A problem that I identified some time ago with young students in New York was that at the age of 18 many came off their parents' health insurance. Some may have extensions to the age of 20 or until after college. Others, however, have no insurance cover and there have been tragedies where people have not gone for treatment early enough because of worries over cost. I would therefore favour the setting-up of government-sponsored health centres for young people. As the minimum age of marriage in most states is 15, it would seem sensible for such centres to cater for the 15–25 age range. They could deal with the whole range of problems experienced by young people during this crucial period of their lives.

Apart from the problems with health insurance, we have seen that there are gaps between parents and children in terms of communication, which these centres could help to overcome. Young people have high risks of automobile and motorcycle accidents and also certain kinds of drug-related problems which could be helped by such centres. In terms of sexuality, I would see the centres as presenting the alternative views on premarital sex but there would be pregnancy testing and birth control services for those who needed them. These would be offered free as part of general health care. This kind of step would help to prevent the problems associated with young pregnancies and reduce the demand for abortion. It would also bring the United States services more into line with those of other countries that are worse off in financial terms but still manage to attain better average levels of health as measured by the usual indicators.

Changes in the quality of relationships

I have maintained that the recognition of sexuality is a precondition for the use of birth control – if couples are unable to recognise the fact that they are going to have sex, they can hardly plan which methods of birth control they are going to use during it. It seems that one reason for the Dutch rate of unwanted pregnancies being so low is that the fact that the double sexual standard is not so marked. As long ago as 1973 I published the results of a student survey comparing attitudes to sex in Britain and Holland. The report contrasted the two countries and commented: 'The evidence does seem to suggest that there is equality of standards in Holland, at least among students' (*Holland Herald*, May 1973, p. 9). This observation was based on the survey results and was somewhat qualified on the basis of later participant observation. None the less, there was clearly greater sex equality in Holland than there was in Britain at the time.

I have always believed that a movement towards sexual equality benefits both sexes, and it is heartening to see that some positive changes have occurred in recent years. For example, we know that fathers have become increasingly involved with caring for their children. Jackson (1984) reported that in Britain between 1965 and 1975 the percentage of British children read to by their father in the previous week rose from 35 per cent to 47 per cent (although the latter figure was still well below the figure for women, which rose from 48 per cent to 72 per cent over the same period, which prompted Jackson to suggest that men were ten years behind).

It is disappointing that the feminists have not encouraged men to become involved with the movement for sex equality to a greater degree. The movement for the Equal Rights Amendment has ground to a halt in the United States; if more men had been encouraged to join in and help there might have been greater success. Furthermore, highly visible feminists like Germaine Greer and Betty Friedan have been writing books that the media have portrayed as abandoning their earlier values. In the spring 1985 edition of the journal of the leading anti-abortion movement in Britain there is an article that applauds much of what Germaine Greer has to say.

I feel it is time for a more even-handed approach from those involved in the movement for sex equality, with no discrimination on the grounds of race, class or sex. In fact, I have always believed that men who have played traditional roles have been more restricted than their 'feminine' partners. I understand the objections of women to being treated as sex objects rather than being valued as people. However, the other side of that coin is that from a very young age men are given a very poor image of their bodies. They are taught that little boys are made of 'slugs and snails and puppy dogs' tails' instead of 'sugar and spice and all things nice'. They are taught that it is women's bodies that are the source of beauty, while theirs are just potential sources of indecent exposure. Women may be taught to hide their feelings of aggression, and this may lead them to being unable to express themselves: however, the greater socialisation of men into toughness and hiding their feelings may have more important long-term consequences. After studying the reaction of men to the birth of their first child, Jackson commented that he found he was sometimes the only person to whom the man had spoken his feelings and that: 'The image I take away is of men in tears at the birth, and yet feeling they had to disguise them' (1984, p.134).

Provision of abortions

Chapters 2 and 3 have shown that it is impossible to eliminate abortion by imposing legal restrictions. An unwanted pregnancy is such a traumatic experience that women will go great distances, take enormous risks and use up large parts of their savings to get abortions. The banning of abortions in one place only leads to an increase in illegal abortions or to many women, especially the rich, travelling elsewhere. For example:

British women went to France in the early part of the twentieth century and French women came to Britain in great numbers in the mid 1970's. Swedish women went to Poland, New Zealand women went to Australia and up to 1970 American women came to Britain. After 1970 Canadian women went in great numbers to New York State, and after the United States imposed restrictions on financial help for the poor, some women sought cheaper abortions in Mexico. German and Belgian women go to Holland and increasingly Spanish and Irish women come to England. [Francome, 1984a, p.222]

So, making abortion illegal will clearly not solve the problem. In fact it seems likely that in Britain over the period 1896–1914 or in the United States during the 1920s and 1930s abortion was more common than at any other period.

Since this time, improvements in birth control services have greatly reduced abortion numbers. However, as abortion is obviously going to be with us for the foreseeable future, it needs to be provided in the most efficient manner. This book has identified a number of problems that need to be considered.

In Britain, there clearly needs to be some impetus to help improve NHS provision. We have seen that abortions in Britain occur later than in the United States because of bureaucratic delays. Some people feel that this is because the US service is largely privately owned. However, the Italian experience indicates that other factors must be involved. In Italy, women were given the right to choose in May 1978 and in 1979 the Health Service performed 188,000 legal abortions – more than three times the number carried out on the NHS each year. A doctor at one of the London teaching hospitals explained to me why some women at his hospital were in for three days having an abortion: 'The consultant likes to book them in and see them again before they go home. He sees them on the Tuesday, they have the operation on the Wednesday and then he does not go round again until Thursday.' With costs of hospital beds being so high and with there being such a pressure on space and waiting lists it is clear that a change in practice is desirable to save time for everyone.

One innovation that would save money and time in the long

run would be the setting-up of day care units in each of the fourteen Regional Health Authorities in England, with women being able to refer themselves. This would cut out the delays in seeing the first doctor, in waiting for the pregnancy test and in waiting for an appointment with a consultant – all of which we have seen are important problem areas. As I reported in Chapter 4, some areas have negotiated agency agreements with the major charities, whereby the local health authority pays for the abortion but it is carried out in a specialist unit. There are several advantages to this. First, the staff are highly committed to their work and very experienced. One of the problems with abortion in the general service is that many people, while not strongly enough opposed to abortion to opt out on the grounds of conscience as they are clearly allowed to do under the 1967 Act, are nevertheless not too keen on the operation. In such cases, care may not always be at the highest level. There are also sometimes problems of women having abortions placed next to those who are about to have babies or who have problems of infertility. These kinds of difficulties could be eliminated by specialist units.

In the United States, there have been attempts to restrict the number of abortions by removing funding. The evidence of this book suggests that this is not the most effective approach. Rather than forcing women to have children they do not want, the changes should be geared towards preventing unwanted pregnancies.

Appendix

Letter given to respondents

Dear Patient,

This questionnaire is part of a study which hopes to help us learn more about women who need abortion – a task that has never been thoroughly done in this country. We hope that women will tell us some things about their lives and their contact with birth control so that we can plan more efficient services.

We are asking for help from women chosen at random from many different places in a variety of areas. We hope to compare what we learned when a similar survey was carried out in the United States.

Some of the questions are of a very personal nature, but they are a great help in deciding how we should plan for the future, and you can be assured that the questionnaire will be anonymous. There is no need to write your name.

You may find that not all the questions apply to you.

We look forward to receiving your questionnaire.

Confidential questionnaire

There is no need to write your name

1) Age .... years.
2) Who do you live with? *(please circle)*   husband   parents   boyfriend   boyfriend and others   alone   with friends   with your in-laws   others *(please specify)* ....

3) Are you, married single widowed separated divorced ? *(please circle)*

4) What is your occupation? ....

5) What is your mother's occupation, (if any)? ....

6) What is your father's occupation, (if any)? ....

7) In which of the following racial groups would you place yourself? *(please circle)* Black White Asian Hispanic Other, *(please specify)* ....

8) In which town and country do you live? ....

9) What is your religious preference? ....

10) Have you been to a place of worship recently? *(please circle)* past week past two weeks past month past year not in the past year

11) Have you had any previous abortions? If so, please specify how many ....

12) When you had your first menstrual period, had anyone told you what to expect? If so, who? ....

13) How old were you when you had your first period? .. years

14) When you had your first sexual intercourse,

   A) How old were you? .... years

   B) How old was your partner? .... years

   C) What was his relationship to you? *(please circle)* casual boyfriend steady boyfriend husband to be other ....

   D) Did you or your partner use any method of birth control? If so, what method? Pill IUD/coil Cap (Diaphragm) Condom Withdrawal Safe period a Suppository Foam Douching Other ....

15) How many of the following do you think would know that you have had intercourse *(please circle)* father mother brother sister girlfriend religious leader teacher boyfriend no one other ....

16) How many of the following have you discussed birth control with, (if any)? no one father mother brother sister girlfriend religious leader teacher boyfriend/husband other ....

17) How many of the following have you told about your pregnancy, (if any)? father mother no one brother sister girlfriend religious leader teacher boyfriend/husband other ....

18) At the time you became pregnant were you, or your partner, *(please circle)* thinking of using a birth control method using a method sometimes   always using a method not using a method

19) There are many reasons why people do not use birth control. *Please circle* those of the following which apply to you, (if any):   thought sterile   had intercourse unexpectedly could not afford the cost   did not know of any did not know where to go   intended to use but had not made an appointment   religion says it is wrong stopped because of side effects   hoped pregnancy would lead to marriage   did not intend to have intercourse anymore   other reasons *(please specify)* ....

20) If you think you became pregnant because of contraceptive failure, which method did you use? *(please circle)*   Pill IUD/Coil   Cap (Diaphragm)   Condom   Withdrawal Safe Period   Suppository   Foam   Douching Other ....

21) If there are any further comments you would like to make, please write them below: ....
....
....
....
....
....
....

– Thank you very much for your help –

Bibliography

Acton, W. (1878), *Prostitution*, 2nd edn (Frank Cass).

Alberman, E. and Dennis, K. J. (1984), *Late Abortions in England and Wales* (Royal College of Obstetricians and Gynaecologists).

Allcorn, D. (1955), 'The Social Development of Young Men in an English Industrial Suburb' (unpublished PhD thesis, Manchester University).

Allen, I. (1985), *Counselling Services for Sterilisation, Vasectomy and Termination of Pregnancy* (Policy Studies Institute).

Ashton, J. R. (1978), *The Attitudes of Wessex Women Obtaining Abortions outside Their Own Region* (University of Southampton).

Bachrach, C. A. (1984), 'Contraceptive practice among American women, 1973–1982', *Family Planning Perspectives*, vol. 16, no. 6 (Nov/Dec), pp.253–9.

Baird, Sir D. (1973), 'The obstetrician and society', *Journal of Biosocial Science*, Supplement 3, pp.93–111.

Besant, A. (1877), *Law of Population* (Freethought Publishing).

Birkett, W. N. (1939), *Report of the Inter-Departmental Committee on Abortion* (HMSO).

Birth-Rate Commission (1917), *The Declining Birth Rate*, 2nd edn (Chapman and Hall).

BMA (1936), 'Report of the Committee on Medical Aspects of Abortion' *British Medical Journal* (25 April) pp.230–8.

Bunker, J. P. (1970), 'Surgical manpower', *New England Journal of Medicine*, vol. 282, no. 3, pp.135–44.

Bury, J. (1984), *Teenage Pregnancy in Britain* (Birth Control Trust).

Calderone, M. (1958), *Abortion in the United States* (Paul Hoeber Inc.).

Carmen, A. and Moody, H. (1973), *Abortion Counselling and Social Change* (Judson Press).

Cavadino, P. (1976), 'Illegal abortion and the Abortion Act 1967', *British Journal of Criminology*, vol. 16, no. 1, pp.63–7.

Chambers, J. (1981), *Why Late Abortions?* (Birth Control Trust).

Chambers, J. (1984), *Men, Sex and Contraception* (Birth Control Trust/Family Planning Association).

Chen, A. J., Emmanuel, F. C., Ling, S. L. and Kwa, S. B. (1985), 'Legalised abortion. The Singapore experience', *Studies in Family Planning*, vol. 16, no. 3, May/June, pp. 170–8.

Chesser, E. (1950), 'The law of abortion', *Medical World*, vol. 72, p. 495.

Clarke, L., Farrell, C. and Beaumont, B. (1983), *Camden Abortion Study* (British Pregnancy Advisory Service).

Dennis, N., Henriques, P. and Slaughter, C. (1956), *Coal Is Our Life* (Tavistock).

Elderton, E. M. (1914), *Report on the English Birthrate* (Eugenics Society).

Family Planning Association (1984), *The Family Planning Association 'Men Too' Project* (FPA).

Family Planning Information Service (1984a), *Contraceptive Usage in the U.K.*, Fact Sheet C2.

Family Planning Information Service (1984b), *Teenage Pregnancies*, Fact Sheet F1 (Family Planning Association).

Farrell, C. (1978), *My Mother Said* (Routledge & Kegan Paul).

Francome, C. (1976a), 'Youth and Society' (unpublished MA thesis, University of Kent, Canterbury).

Francome, C. (1976b), 'How many illegal abortions?', *British Journal of Criminology*, vol. 16, no. 4, pp.389–92.

Francome, C. (1977), 'Estimating the number of illegal abortions', *Journal of Biosocial Science*, vol. 9, pp.467–79.

Francome, C. (1979), 'More teenage sex', *Breaking Chains*, no. 11, January.

Francome, C. (1980), *Birth Control: A Way Forward* (Marie Stopes House).

Francome, C. (1982), *Gallup on Abortion* (Abortion Law Reform Association/Doctors for a Woman's Choice on Abortion).

Francome, C. (1983), 'Unwanted pregnancies amongst teenagers', *Journal of Biosocial Science*, vol. 15, no. 2.

Francome, C. (1984a), *Abortion Freedom* (Allen & Unwin).

Francome, C. (1984b), 'Teenage pregnancy', *Novum* (May).

Francome, C. (1984c), 'Historical view of the safe period', *Breaking Chains* (April), p.7.

Francome, C. and Francome, C. (1979), 'Towards an understanding of the American abortion rate', *Journal of Biosocial Science*, Vol. 11, pp.303–13.

Frank, P. I., Kay, C. R., Wingrave, S. J., Lewis, T. L. T., Osborne, J. and Newell, C. (1985), 'Induced abortion operations and their early sequelae', *Journal of the Royal College of General Practitioners* (April), pp.175–80.

Friedan, B. (1963), *The Feminine Mystique* (W. W. Norton).

Gilder, G. (1981), *Wealth and Poverty* (Basic Books).

Ginoff, H. G. (1969), *Between Parent and Teenager* (Macmillan).

Glass, D. V. (1940), *Population Policies and Movements in Europe* (Frank Cass).

Goode, W. J. (1964), *The Family* (Prentice Hall).

Goodhart, C. B. (1964), 'The frequency of illegal abortion', *Eugenics Review*, vol. 55, p.197.

Goodhart, C. B. (1969), 'Estimation of illegal abortion', *Journal of Biosocial Science*, vol. 1, p.235.

Goodhart, C. B. (1973), 'On the incidence of illegal abortion', *Population Studies*, vol. 27, pp.207–34.

Gordon, L. (1977), *Women's Body, Women's Right* (Penguin).

Hale, E. M. (1860), *On the Homeopathic Treatment of Abortion*.

Henshaw, S. K. (1985), personal communication (to be published by AGI).

Henshaw, S. K., Binkin, N. J., Blaine, E. and Smith, J. (1985), 'A portrait of American women who obtain abortions', *Family Planning Perspectives*, vol. 17, no. 2, pp.90–6.

Hindell, K. and Simms, M. (1971), *Abortion Law Reformed* (Peter Owen).

Hodge, H. L. (1854), *Criminal Abortion* (T. K. & P. G. Collins).

Hollick, F. (1849), *Diseases of Women, Their Causes and Cure Familiarly Explained* (New York).

Hollingshead, A. B. (1949), *Elmstown Youth*, First Science edition, 1961.

Home Office (1984), *Criminal Statistics England and Wales* (HMSO).

Jackson, B. (1984), *Fatherhood* (Allen & Unwin).

Kennedy, L. (1971), *Ten Rillington Place* (Panther).

Kinsey, A., Pomeroy, W. B., Martin, C. E. and Gebhard, P. H. (1953), *The Sexual Behavior of the Human Female* (W. B. Saunders and Co.).

Lambert, J. (1971), 'Survey of 3,000 unwanted pregnancies', *British Medical Journal*, vol. 4, p.156.

Lea, J. and Young, J. (1985), *What Is To Be Done about Law and Order?* (Penguin).

Linner, B. (1968), *Sex and Society in Sweden* (Cape).

Luker, K. (1975), *Taking Chances* (University of California Press).

Luker, K. (1984), *Abortion and the Politics of Motherhood* (University of California Press).

Malinowski, B. (1929), *The Sexual Life of Savages* (Routledge).

Mead, M. (1944), *The American Troops and the British Community* (Hutchinson).

Means, C. (1968), 'The law of New York concerning abortion and the status of the fetus 1664–1968: a case of cessation of constitutionality', *New York Law Forum*, vol. 14, pp.411–515.

Means, C. (1970), in Robert Hall, *Abortion in a Changing World* (Association for the Study of Abortion).

Means, C. (1971), 'The phoenix of abortion freedom', *New York Law Forum*, vol. 17, p.335–410.

Mohr, J. C. (1978), *Abortion in America* (Oxford University Press).

OPCS (1980), *Labour Force Survey 1973, 1975 and 1977* (HMSO).

OPCS (1983), *Abortion Statistics 1981*, Series AB, No 8 (HMSO).

OPCS (1984), *Abortion Statistics 1982*, Series AB, No 9 (HMSO).

OPCS (1985), *Abortion Statistics 1983*, Series AB, No 10 (HMSO).

Parish, T. N. (1935), 'A thousand cases of abortion', *Journal of Obstetrics and Gynaecology of the British Empire* (December).

Parry, L. A. (1932), *Criminal Abortion* (Bale, Carswell).

Pomeroy, H. S. (1888), *Ethics of Marriage* (Funk and Wagnalls).

Potts, M., Diggory, P. and Peel, J. (1970), 'Preliminary assessment of the 1967 Abortion Act in practice', *Lancet*, vol. i, p.287.

Potts, M., Diggory, P. and Peel, J. (1977), *Abortion* (Cambridge University Press).

Pratt, W. F., Mosher, W. D., Bachrach, C. A. and Horn, M. C. (1984), *Understanding U.S. Fertility* (Population Reference Bureau Inc.).

Reed, J. (1978), *From Private Vice to Public Virtue* (Basic Books).

Registrar General Scotland (1984), *Annual Report 1983* (HMSO).

Roberts, K. (1985), *Youth and Leisure* (Allen & Unwin).

Rongy, A. J. (1933), *Abortion: Legal or Illegal* (Vanguard).

Ross, E. (1907), 'Western civilisation and the birth rate', *American Journal of Sociology* (March), pp.607–29.

Royal Commission on Population (1949), *Report*, Cmnd 7695 (HMSO).

Sanger, M. (1915), *Family Limitation* (Rose Witcop).

Sanger, M. (1938), *My Fight for Birth Control* (W. W. Norton).

Schofield, M. (1965), *The Sexual Behaviour of Young People* (Longmans).

Shostak, A. B., McLouth, G. with Seng, L. (1984), *Men and Abortion* (Praeger).

Simms, M. (1975), 'The compulsory pregnancy lobby, then and now', *Journal of the Royal College of Medical Practitioners*, vol. 25, p. 716.

Simpson, F. (1985), 'Gillick judgement', *Breaking Chains*, no. 41 (October).

Stopes, M. C. C. (1918), *Married Love* (The Critic and Guide Company).

Storer, H. R. (1866), *Why Not? A Book for Every Woman* (Lee and Shepard).

Taussig, F. J. (1910), *Prevention and Treatment of Abortion* (George Keemer and Co.).

Taussig, F. J. (1936), *Abortion – Spontaneous and Induced* (C. V. Mosby).

Tietze, C. (1983), *Induced Abortion*, 5th edn (Population Council).

Toner, B. (1982), *The Facts of Rape* (Arrow Books).

US Department of Commerce (1983), *Statistical Abstract of the United States* (Bureau of Census).

Waller, W. (1937), 'The rating and dating complex', *American Sociological Review*, vol. 2, pp. 727–34.

Whitehouse, B. (1932), 'Indications for the induction of abortion', *British Medical Journal*, 20 August, pp. 337–41.

Wilson, E. (1983), *What Is To Be Done About Violence Against Women* (Penguin).

Wimperis, V. (1960), *The Unmarried Mother and Her Child* (Allen & Unwin).

Woodside, M. (1963), 'Attitudes of women abortionists', *Howard Journal*, vol. 11, p. 93.

Index